Pagan Portals

Iris

Goddess of the Rainbow and Messenger of the Godds

Pagan Portals

Iris

Goddess of the Rainbow and
Messenger of the Godds

Irisanya Moon

MOON
BOOKS

Winchester, UK
Washington, USA

JOHN HUNT PUBLISHING

First published by Moon Books, 2021
Moon Books is an imprint of John Hunt Publishing Ltd., No. 3 East Street, Alresford
Hampshire SO24 9EE, UK
office@jhpbooks.net
www.johnhuntpublishing.com
www.moon-books.net

For distributor details and how to order please visit the 'Ordering' section on our website.

Text copyright: Irisanya Moon 2021

ISBN: 978 1 78904 711 0
978 1 78904 712 7 (ebook)
Library of Congress Control Number: 2021930338

Design: Matthew Greenfield

UK: Printed and bound by CPI Group (UK) Ltd, Croydon, CR0 4YY
Printed in North America by CPI GPS partners

We operate a distinctive and ethical publishing philosophy in all areas of our business, from our global network of authors to production and worldwide distribution.

Contents

Acknowledgements

I want to thank and acknowledge so many people in my life for helping me get to this point. It's not always been easy, nor has it always been clear what I'm meant to do next. But I have understanding friends, helpful mentors, and ongoing signs from the universe.

From the rainbows that dropped from the sky during momentous decisions and to the whispers of the godds as I woke up from sleep. I presence these moments and these times when a lack of clarity could have stopped me and could have caused me to turn away.

Thank you to the signs. To the wonders. To the surrender. More specifically, I give thanks to Copper Persephone, my mentor and friend. She not only helped me remember my power, but also to claim it. She was the human who was always there for me, encouraging me and helping me to come back to my heart. She passed away in June of 2020, during a year of so many losses. In her last days, I felt her call out that everything would be okay, that she would be there -- no matter what happened. She is one of the reasons I teach. And she is one of the few people who knew I wanted to write this book. I am so grateful for her. What is remembered, lives.

I also give thanks to my ever-patient friends, who listen to me perseverate about how I won't be able to write anything or that I won't have anything to say. I sometimes don't know why you continue to listen and encourage me, but I'm glad that you do. I love you all. I am blessed to have such precious beings in my life. I want to include a list here, but I don't want to leave anyone out in a moment of forgetfulness.

I am also so grateful to Moon Books and Trevor Greenfield. I've said it before and I'll say it again, thank you for believing in a writer you've never met. I hope we can rectify that soon. Please know that your kind words and well-timed support has helped me realize a childhood dream several times over. And I know we're just at the start of what's to emerge.

Of course, I thank Iris. I didn't know you were a being until you presented yourself to me. I had no idea that you were such a strong messenger in my life until I listened. I am now listening more closely to your words, to your blessings, and to your visions. My hope is that while you may be a minor figure in literature, you become a major figure in the lives of those who need to hear and bring the messages of the godds. Or just to listen to what is already being brought into presence.

Hail Iris. Hail Beloved One and namesake. I took on your name because you arrived right when I needed to hear you. Taking on your name was and is an act of embodiment and a ritual of dedication. While we might look away from each other at times, we also come back. May we always come back.

Author's Note

One thing that I'd like to make clear before this book continues is that my experience of the godds* is my experience. I am clear that there is no 'one way' to experience the divine or mystery or whatever you decide to call this. Though you might have a way of relating to the godds that I don't understand, it doesn't make it any less valid or true.

While I might offer ways to relate with Iris, you might not find they all resonate with you. That's fine. I might offer something which inspires something completely different -- that's great! If there's anything I can offer to a reader, it's that building relationships with the godds can help bring us closer to ourselves and can help us recognize and claim our power.

Recently, I made the comment that my relationships with the godds are grounded in devotion and communion, not supplication. While I might sit at the feet of the godds and I might give offerings and worship, it is not based in feeling less than divine. Thus, my writing will talk of Iris as a being who I relate to, not look up to. This might not work for you, and that's just fine. But it will likely be helpful to know that before we go much further.

You can apply the way that I relate to the godds to any godd. Really. What I have said about Aphrodite in my previous book, I could say about Hecate or Brigid or Horus, etc. So, if you get inspired by a book to look at other godds in the same way, that's terrific.

My work is the hope that I can inspire a reader, so in building that bridge across from my beliefs and experiences to yours, I offer personal insights, stories, and lenses. I recognize this. I am not someone who looks only to text for meaning and truth. And I also do not hold that there is one personal gnosis for everyone, though I try to assemble the facts I can as a starting point. In the absence of much study on Iris (so far), I will move toward wider interpretations and meanings. I may not consider all of the thoughts of scholars and those who are delighted to write very large books. (Honestly, I may not have seen their thoughts yet.)

So, if there are any historic errors or incorrect facts, they are mine. That said, Iris doesn't have a lot of resources and references as compared to the other Greek godds. While She plays roles in many stories you might know, Her role is often written out or minimized to focus on the 'larger' godds. While considered a minor deity, Iris is certainly the one who moves stories along, who moves lives along, and who comes at precisely the right time. And that is where we begin.

*Note: I will use 'godd' to help move away from gendered words for deity who I believe move beyond human categorization.

Introduction

The true harvest of my daily life is somewhat as intangible and indescribable as the tints of morning or evening. It is a little stardust caught, a segment of the rainbow which I have clutched.
-- Henry David Thoreau

I want to tell you about rainbows. That is where I want to begin. I want to begin with the beautiful images of light that refracts perfectly through a raindrop to project colors on clouds and sky. I could tell you about the process of this, but I have to remember that before science was trying to explain everything, rainbows arrived -- and they were wondrous.

I imagine rainbows to have been signs of something important. They may have come after strong storms or only show up in certain areas of the world where conditions were right. Or they arrived when the sun shone across the sea's waves. Or they fell on a piece of paper when it was in the right place at the right time. And rainbows have become a messenger of so many things: hope, love, diversity, pride, and strength.

Even before you meet Iris (if you haven't met before), I invite you to consider the places where rainbows have already shown up for you. I invite you to think about how rainbows have either brought you peace or brought you brightness. Where have they already shown up? If they haven't or you can't remember, no worries. I imagine they will arrive soon.

The Story of Meeting and Knowing

As with Aphrodite, Iris was a goddess who made a dramatic appearance, one that I could not ignore or pass off as a coincidence. It was 2008. I had been a practicing Witch for about 10 years, had just faced some hard times in my life and decided to go to a thing called Witchcamp in California. It was a Reclaiming event and

1

it was (and still is) a weeklong event with classes, ritual, and community.

I didn't know anyone. I met someone on the way as we drove together with all of our camping gear and luggage. Along the way, she told me of Reclaiming, what I could expect and I took it all in, word by word. There's a stretch of Highway 1 where I can still remember learning about aspecting and about what that looked like in ritual. But this is not the important part of the story. It's only a step along the way.

When I returned from that camp, I was dirty, tattooed, and amazed that magick was real. I had never been in a large ritual and, to the day, I can still remember what happened and how it felt. I continue to chase that feeling in my work as a priestess and Witch. As I returned, I had a series of magickal experiences, even one that led me to Berlin. I was on a work project that allowed me to work for a certain number of hours a day, but then I could return to a flat to have my free time.

During that time, I went to the Pergamon on a day off. I remember walking in when it was under construction or renovation. When I walked in, I was greeted by a series of Greek godds. They were everywhere. And I was taking pictures on my clunky digital camera until the battery died. And while I didn't know it then, I had met Iris.

She is in a relief on the wall today. Beside Hera, as She often was, Iris appears to be leading Zeus' four-horse chariot. The pieces of the relief have mostly been lost to the effects of time, but you could see where Iris might be, though only in one small space.

I've looked back at my pictures, and I think I captured Her, but it is hard to tell. What is important to know is that a month later, I was thinking about my witchcraft and the people I met at camp. I was curious about where I might go next. There were core classes in Reclaiming and they were on the weekends and I had time and money. Still, I wasn't sure. Elements of Magick was scheduled to be taught by Copper Persephone and Diana Melisabee in January of 2009. And I had the registration form in hand. But I wasn't sure. It was a December afternoon and I needed to turn it in because registration was closing that night.

It was overnight in a place I didn't know. It was time away from home. It was with people I didn't know and I was nervous. Would this be a good thing to do? Would I be safe? I sat with the form and looked out the window of my apartment. The widest rainbow I had ever seen was pouring from the sky onto the mountains. Bright and brilliant. Clear and from seemingly nowhere. I don't remember it raining that day. I don't remember anything more than the brightness of that bow. But let's be clear, I still hesitated. After all, that was impressive, but what did it mean? I turned to the internet. I searched for 'goddess of the rainbow' without knowing if that was a thing.

Iris. I made a sound and looked over pages of information. Pages that don't appear today. Information that isn't there today. I know this because I printed out what I found back then and it doesn't look the same today.

- Messenger of the Godds
- Iridescent
- Graceful

I had heard the word 'grace' many times in my life, and while it doesn't seem like a big detail, it hit my heart. People in my life had always (and still do) describe my energy as graceful. I am still slow to believe that, but nonetheless, it has been true. All of the other times, I heard it as a term of 'good' and 'compliant.' This time, I heard it as power and groundedness. And that Iris is a messenger seemed to align with what I did in my work life as a writer. And I gave up a lot of my security to write, leaving a job that hurt me again and again. Trusting that I would know what to do and when to do it. *Maybe I'm a messenger*, I thought.

I wish I could put into words what this meant to me in that moment. I wish I could adequately describe the way my skin flushed and my heart raced. How I felt that it was a mystical push. Because it was not the first time rainbows appeared during a difficult decision. They came when I left a job that was hurting me, the colors arriving as I drove away after dropping off my resignation letter. I wasn't sure about moving across the country – but there were rainbows everywhere the first few years I lived here. Needless to say, after that fateful Internet search, I became clear this was a sign from the godds (according to me). I filled out that registration form. I filled it out and started a journey that brings me to this moment.

What's in a Name?

Because I don't always meet folks in person and they don't hear my name said aloud, I wanted to briefly tell the story of how I came to my name. And yes, it's EYE-ris-AHN-ya.

I had that meeting with Iris, or that encounter or that moment where I realized She could be calling to me. I wasn't sure, but I followed anyway. I realize in this particular moment that just like my relationship with Aphrodite, Iris came into me during aspecting (spiritual possession) and that's when I knew our relationship was real.

I was not Irisanya yet. It was May of 2009. Early in my Reclaiming days I took a mask making class with Copper Persephone. We were tasked with making masks of a deity and then use them later on to learn about aspecting. It would be my first time aspecting. I was not sure if I was ready. I was not sure if that mattered in that moment or if I even considered it. I made a mask of Iris because I realized I didn't know what She looked like. I made it white with a rainbow across the middle and a golden piece of glass at the third eye. It felt right to me and I still have it to this day.

At some point before we aspected, one of my contact lenses

4

had fallen out so I was unable to see out of one eye. Not the best way to go outside in the dark with a mask on and let a deity enter my body for the first time. But as soon as Iris entered my body, as soon as I invited Her in, I could see. I could see up the dark path and I could travel with ease. There were many people in aspect, but Iris floated around and simply enjoyed the nature and the chill of the night. When the aspecting was done, I couldn't see clearly out of that eye anymore. She helped me see.

It was around then that I started to wonder if I could take on Her name. I didn't have a magickal name at that point and it was becoming important to me to have one. So, I sat down and tried to work out what my name might be. Iris. That seemed too simple. My birth name includes a 'y' that makes it unique, so I wanted to include that. Irisania. No. Irisanya. Hmm. I looked up what 'anya' meant to be sure. "Inexhaustible energy." That fit too. Was it too easy?

I liked the way it sounded. I liked the way that it felt when I saw it. And it was a sacred promise I would be making. Holding this name. Holding this energy. So, I held that name in myself and used it as the anchor in my magickal practice. The home base when I was away from myself. I used it when I ran energy through my body via the Iron Pentacle and when I worked in magickal spaces on my own. I kept repeating it to myself and carrying it to see how it felt. I am pretty sure I was sharing it with people at that point, but time is funny and vague.

What I do know is that I took on the name as my own in February of 2010 during a ritual where my coven at the time was almost swept out to the ocean after walking down to a secluded beach. Iris has guided me here. To this place. To sharing Her with you too.

Why Iris, Why Now

Before we get into what Iris seems to be about for me and for the research I have done, I want to presence the question why is she important now? I have a few thoughts about this. And I'm sure you're here because of other thoughts. Or maybe some of the same.

Iris to me is the being that has been out and about in society without a lot of recognition. As mentioned before, there aren't a lot of stories that talk about Her for more than a few lines. She isn't someone who gets brought into a lot of conversations about Greek practices. And She actually doesn't appear to have any books about Her at this present moment.

She reached out to me to tell Her stories and to bring my experience to a reader as an offering because the world needs to remember the godds in all of their forms. In all of their roles. In all of their service. And in doing so, readers and seekers will remember and recognize they too have roles, however big or small, to play. She wants to remind us that we are not alone. That there are messages everywhere if only we are willing to listen. She shows up in so many ways, on so many days, offering us what we need -- though not always what we want.

Iris shows me the value of service and traveling in liminal spaces. She is a goddess who moves from the heavens to the River Styx and back again. And even if you're not sure what that means or how that applies to you, She wants to show you the value of movement and moving between the here and there. Of flying and of knowing you can traverse through all of the places your life takes you.

But most importantly, Iris offers a message of hope. In this world of conflict and corruption, oppression and war, She is the one who brings the truth that we are a resilient people. Hope is not a thing that is guaranteed, to be sure, but it is a part of our lives we can remember. Iris helps me remember that there is light beyond the storm. There is beauty in breakdowns. There are times to shine and times to simply serve. She is the reminder of being optimistic about whatever comes next, even dangerously so. While She knows the goings-on of the godds,

She also delivers those messages in ways that people can hear them clearly. So that even the godds listen.

I recognize that with so little literature on Iris, much of my writing is informed by my own personal gnosis, but I want to make sure to invite you to do the same. Who is She to you? This might all sound vague at first. It is. It is different for everyone. It will be different for you and for the person next to you. And that is a blessing. That is the start of a spell only you can create and conjure and bring into form. Iris shows up today because we need to listen more. Let us stop, steady, and hear.

Chapter 1

Meeting Iris

*Soaring to heaven on balanced wings, [Iris] blazed a rainbow trail
beneath the clouds as she flew ... ... Iris, glory of the sky,
cloud-borne.*
-- Virgil, Aeneid 9. 2 ff.

Welcome to a rainbow path, the way of opening and hearing
and knowing and listening, the way of taking things in and
becoming a messenger too. No matter why you are here and
no matter what you feel you are called to next, I welcome you
and Iris welcomes you here too. In this journey or even in this
exploration before a journey, there are no promises to be made.
There are no vows you need to have ready to begin. Bring only
your heart and your willingness to listen. And I want to be clear
that listening is not just something you do with your ears. You
can listen with your heart, your skin, your gut, your mind, and,
really, any part of you that senses messages.

While we will talk more about building relationships later
on, I want to begin with an initial meeting with Iris to set the
proverbial stage for encountering Her. Notice that I do use 'Her'
to reference Iris because that is how She shows up for me, but you
might use a different pronoun, which is perfectly okay. (I also
capitalize Her pronouns when I write about Her, as that works
for me. That said, when writing about Iris, I do not capitalize the
pronouns for other godds to minimize confusion.)

What is important at this point is to open up to what I might
offer, but leave room for your own interpretation. Leave room
for your own knowing and your own wisdom. No godd is
completely one way because humans have different eyes and
different experiences through which they might perceive. Be

open to it all.

That is not to say that Iris is everything to everyone, nor is any deity, in my experience. But I just want to offer flexibility or even permission, if needed, to have your own experience alongside what I offer in this book. I am not interested in telling you how to do anything or how to be with a beloved of mine. I only know that if you are called to Iris, that you are here because of not only who She is, but also who you are. This will make more sense as we move on.

Forget perfection and forget learning it all in this moment or even this week or month or year. Bring your willingness and your openness. Bring the wings of your wonder and the stretch of your heart.

Stop: Why are You Called?

To me, it is maddening to have a spiritual and often emotional experience and then someone asks me to describe my motivations. Sometimes things just happen. Sometimes I just have a feeling or an idea. Sometimes, you just fall in love because you do, right? When it comes to being human, it is messy and complicated and often confusing. One day, something makes perfect sense and the next, you're not sure why you thought that in the first place.

While I will still find explaining myself to be maddening, and you never have to, I do find my work with deities to be more effective when I get clear about my 'why.' Why am I here? Why do I think I was called to this work?

And I don't know your answer. It might be unclear. (And that's okay too.) But I invite you to drop into the question. Why are you called to Iris? You may have already heard messages or you have studied Her and realized that She might have something to give to you. You may feel She can teach you something or help you with something that pains you right now. This might be a list of items or explanations. And before you move onto the next section, I would encourage you to complete this list, even if it's unfinished.

Steady: Release Expectation

Did you make a list that helps define your 'why'? Great. I think the most important part of this question is what it alludes to: expectations. Do you have expectations in this journey? Do you have conditions that mean it's 'good' or 'bad'?

Unspoken expectations are premeditated resentments is something I saw on the Internet a while ago. (I've found it attributed to John A. Johnson, PhD, as well as random memes.) While this was posted to show the way that our unsaid expectations can damage interpersonal relationships, I think this applies to deities as well. What are you expecting from Iris? What are you expecting from yourself? I encourage you to write this down and keep it somewhere you can find it in the future. When you get lost along the way or you're not sure why you feel blocked or stuck, you can look back at this and see what your expectations were.

I truly believe I need to drop my expectations in order to be truly present in a relationship. Because I am whoever I am in a moment and the person I'm with is who they are, I need to meet that moment without expectation. I need to meet a relationship with clear communication of what I expect as this allows the other to tell me if this is possible. And if it's not possible, it allows me to make a decision to live with that or to find another who can meet that expectation. Not all deities are going to be the right fit for us. Some are going to be casual acquaintances and others will be lifelong partners in magick. Getting clear on that now will help you move ahead.

Hear: The Messages are Everywhere

Once you begin to get clear about your 'why' and your expectations, you will have a better understanding of how you arrive to meet Iris. You will know why you have showed up and what Iris might have to offer you. From this place of tapping into deeper knowing, my experience tells me that messages begin to arrive. Or they become clearer and easier to notice.

One of my favorite practices for messages is to be out in nature or out in a place where I feel at ease. I have a daily practice of walking around my neighborhood and not listening to anything. I also go by myself because I just want to be with who I am that day. Sometimes, I talk to myself about everyday things or about important things. Sometimes, I have conversations with other people (in my mind) in advance of us actually talking in person. During these times, I notice messages and sounds. For example, I might have heard a hawk when I was talking about how to approach a difficult conversation. Or I might see a rainbow right when I was talking about something else. I look around. I feel how my body is. Am I tense? Am I relaxed? How does the outside inform my inside landscape? Are there messages there? What do I see around me?

I also tend to write down experiences I have, dreams I have, and other strange occurrences. I might be talking to a friend who is talking about something and uses the same words that I used in a conversation at the same time.

I try to collect it all. In doing so, I can go back and see trends. I can see where certain signs and sounds or feelings showed up. I can see that this means _____. And then I can look out for those specific signs when I need help in another situation.

If you're not someone who goes outside or feels safe going outside, you might also turn to divination tools. I personally like simple things -- turning on a radio station to see what song is playing or opening a book to find a passage that seems to jump out or drawing a tarot card to see what the picture tells me.

Messages are everywhere. Collect as many as you can, even the ones that don't seem to make any sense. Those are often the ones that tend to be the most telling since they can't be easy to discern at first glance. I call this practice chasing rainbows. We'll use more specific practices in later chapters.

Practice: Trance into the Realm of Iris

Even if you haven't had a chance to move through the last part to figure out why you're here or you're not sure, I offer a trance to help you move into a meeting with Iris. I think of this as having tea with deity since it is an opportunity to sense into each other. As though you're making small talk on a train. No pressure. Just an experience.

You can choose to read this and follow the words into a trance state, or you can record yourself reading this section to help you let go a bit more easily. To prepare, get into a space that is comfortable and where you will not be disturbed for a little while. You can choose to lay down or sit or stand, depending on what your body needs to feel safe and present, and preferably not sleepy. That said, many of my teachers told me that falling asleep during trance was still doing the work.

I invite you to close your eyes if that feels right for you or keep them slightly open with a soft gaze. For those that enjoy following their breath, I invite you to witness your breath as it is right now. How it moves in and out of your lungs. There is no need to change it or fix it. Be where you are right now.

And if the breath is not a place of comfort for you, I invite you to find a texture on your body that you can touch to bring yourself present. Or you can focus on a part of your body that feels good and calm.

Allow yourself to be in the place you are, wherever you are in this moment. Focus on what calms you and grounds you, allowing the rest of the world to move further and further away. Drop your awareness down to the tips of your toes and then allow it to travel up the space of ankle and calf to your knee. Notice what's there and allow it to be as it is. And allow anything that doesn't need to be here right now to drop, to sink, to fall away.

Bring that awareness up to the space of your thighs and up to your hips, swirling around in your pelvic bowl. Notice what's there and allow it to be as it is. And allow anything that doesn't need to be here right now to drop, to sink, to fall away.

Feel your awareness rise up to the space of your gut and stomach, to that place of power, will, digestion, and heat. Moving up to the space of your rib cage that holds your precious lungs and heart. And settle on your courageous heart. Notice what's there and allow it to be as it is. And allow anything that doesn't need to be here right now to drop, to sink, to fall away.

And as your awareness rises again, along the space of collarbones and shoulders, down each arm to elbow and wrist and each fingertip. Notice what's there and allow it to be as it is. And allow anything that doesn't need to be here right now to drop, to sink, to fall away. Then your awareness comes to the space of your throat and along your jawbone. To the space of your cheeks and eyes and to your forehead. Moving up to the top of your head and the space that was soft when you were born. Notice what's there and allow it to be as it is. And allow anything that doesn't need to be here right now to drop, to sink, to fall away.

Take a moment here to feel the way your body feels. That which doesn't need to be present has sunk into the earth where it might be transformed into something more nourishing.

From this place, I invite you to widen and expand your witch's eye, your magical eye, your inner wisdom and knowing. Allow it to stretch until you can feel, see, and sense further than you could before. In this new wide expanse, you begin to be aware of a path that calls to you, that knows your name. And you begin to make your way.

Perhaps by flying or walking or slithering or floating, each moment moves you closer to a space that feels like it holds godds. What does it look like? What does it feel like? What do you notice and sense? In that space, an iridescent figure begins to arrive with features that sharpen and reveal. It is Iris in the form that makes the most sense to you. And She has been waiting for you to arrive. Allow yourself to have time with Her and to listen to Her. Even if She doesn't share words, allow your senses to widen and receive whatever happens next.]

To some, She might have wings. To some She shows up in a long, flowing tunic with a rainbow behind Her. Others see Her in a short tunic with winged sandals. Or you might see something different.

(Give a few minutes to have that experience. I usually give about 3 to 5 minutes at first.)

While these moments with Iris are precious, they are also fleeting. We can not stay in the trance space forever, but you can always return in your own time and in your dreams. For now, you can begin to say your goodbyes and ask any last questions before leaving. You may want to offer gratitude for this experience, to Iris.

And you begin to feel the call to return, traveling the same path that you started on, knowing each step so easily and intimately. It is quicker and smoother.

And you return to the top of your head, bringing your awareness closer in to your body. Coming back, back, back to your head and to the forehead and eyes and jawbone and throat.

Back, back, back.

Back into your arms and shoulders and collar bone.

Back, back, back.

Back into your courageous heart and lungs and ribcage.

Back, back, back.

Back into the place of nourishment, digestion, will, power, heat.

Back, back, back.

Back into the place of pelvic bowl, hips, and thighs.

Back, back, back.

Back into the knees, calves, ankles, and toes -- and back, back, BACK.

Allow yourself to come back into your body. It can help to touch and pat down the edges of your body to feel where you are in this moment. You might want to say your name out loud a few times. Or you might want to drink some water, have a salty snack, or get up and move around to bring yourself present again. Take some time to write down your thoughts about what happened. They don't have to make sense, as you can return to them later.

This practice of going into trance can help you move beyond your logical mind. The mind that wants to explain everything. This trance technique is more about opening up to experience versus having a certain experience. That said, you could do this over and over and get different experiences. And we'll have other meditations and experiences for different aspects of Iris.

For now, stop and think about where you're at and how you might be impacted by your experience of Iris at this point. Do you have new messages and new expectations? Do you have a sense of where this journey might take you next? What did She tell you and what did She already show you?

And if you didn't get a clear message or have a clear journey. That's okay too. I don't think of this as a stop sign, but rather a moment to reflect about how you feel. If you're frustrated, try again. You haven't done anything wrong. Just try again. Or try a meditative practice that works better for you.

Chapter 2

Stories of Iris

Sokrates (Socrates): He who said that Iris (Rainbow) was the child of Thaumas (Wonder) made a good genealogy.
-- Plato, Theaetetus 155d (trans. Lamb), Greek philosopher C4th B.C.

Born of Thaumas (a marine godd) and Elektra (a cloud nymph), according to most texts, Iris is the sister of the Harpies. She has many epithets in texts, including Khrysopteron (golden-winged), Aellôpos (storm-footed), Roscida (dewy), and Thaumantias/ Thaumantos (Thaumas' daughter). According to multiple sources, She is married to Zephyrus, the godd of the west wind.

The translation of 'Iris' is the rainbow messenger, or the goddess of the rainbow. In Greece, rainbows would span from the clouds to the sea, and it was thought this was where Iris would travel. Known as the messenger of Hera, and even handmaiden, Iris' role is to carry the messages of the godds down to the humans or to other godds.

Some stories say that She would present messages to humans in the form of another being, a friend, or some comforting person. In this way, She was able to interact among both the godds and the humans, as directed by others.

Her role is described as being a messenger, but also a figure that helps to keep peace in the land. Like a rainbow, She disappears as quickly as She appears, bestowing the messages swiftly before leaving again. In some places, She is the rainbow, and in other places, She travels upon the rainbow.

With that, the gracious goddess (Thetis) took a dark-blue shawl ... and set out on her journey, preceded by swift Iris of the storm-swift

feet. The waters of the sea made way for them and they came out on
the shore and darted up to heaven....
-- The Iliad

Iris is also said to be one of the few godds who can travel, at will, between the worlds -- even to the underworld. What is also interesting is that Iris not only serves godds, but She also transports messages of Her own. Over time, She becomes more of the servant of Hera, relied upon to be the obedient messenger, as many godds needed messengers to carry their words.

River Styx

While not a story so much as a purpose, Iris was the one who traveled to the River Styx when the godds were making sacred promises. She would bring Her pitcher and fill it with the water that trickled down from the high rocks. This action and responsibility was not a frequent one, as the godds did not often want to converse or interfere with Styx, but rather Iris would be called to this purpose when the godds were in conflict. While not a direct mediator, the actions of Iris allow for the resolution or at least truce between divine beings.

(ll. 775-806) And there dwells the goddess loathed by the deathless
gods, terrible Styx, eldest daughter of back-flowing
(23) Ocean. She lives apart from the gods in her glorious house
vaulted over with great rocks and propped up to heaven all round
with silver pillars. Rarely does the daughter of Thaumas, swift-
footed Iris, come to her with a message over the sea's wide back.
But when strife and quarrelarise among the deathless gods, and
when any of them who live in the house of Olympus lies, then Zeus
sends Iris to bring in a golden jug the great oath of the gods from
far away, the famous cold water which trickles down from a high
and beetling rock.

This journey is one of the details that surprised me about Iris. After all, it is not common for a godd to travel between all of worlds at free will. While there are stories of moving between realms because of certain tasks or because of certain situations, Iris seems to be a unique being.

As such, there are sources who connect Iris to Hecate, thinking Iris might be closely related since they have similar movements. I'm not sure how I feel about that, but since Hecate is in the story of Persephone and Demeter as trying to help Demeter come back from her rage, I can see how this could be a possible translation and thus interpretation.

Persephone and Demeter

To Demeter: (ll. 301-320) First he
sent golden-winged Iris to call rich-haired Demeter, lovely in
form. So he commanded. And she obeyed the dark-clouded Son of
Cronos, and sped with swift feet across the space between. She came
to the stronghold of fragrant Eleusis, and there finding
dark-cloaked Demeter in her temple, spake to her and uttered
winged words:

(ll. 321-323) Demeter, father Zeus, whose wisdom is everlasting,
calls you to come join the tribes of the eternal gods: come
therefore, and let not the message I bring from Zeus pass
Unobeyed.

(ll. 324-333) Thus said Iris imploring her.

Iris also shows up in the story of Persephone and Demeter as the one who tries to speak to Demeter after Zeus has found out that Demeter has made all of the lands bare in her sorrow for the loss of Persephone to Hades. Zeus finds out that Demeter is in exile, away from her duties in keeping the world in green and growth. After Persephone has been taken (or chooses to go to the underworld, depending on your interpretation), Demeter seems to be furious and out of her mind. She calls to the godds to help her find her daughter, but the godds will not answer. They will not help. After all, the godds are not meant to meddle in the affairs of other godds.

So, Zeus decides that Iris should go to Demeter to tell her to come back to her role and to stop being stuck in her grief and rage. Iris goes to implore Demeter to come back to the realm of the godds. But Demeter does not listen.

Servant of Hera

Because Iris is close to Hera, She is the one who listens and delivers the messages of this godd, and is often described as the most trusted one. While I have interpretations of the stories, I invite you to bring them into you as images, as messages that might offer you something you need to hear too.

Ovid, Metamorphoses 11. 585 (trans. Melville) (Roman epic C1st B.C. to C1st A.D.)

[Hera addresses Iris:] 'Iris, my voice's trustiest messenger, hie quickly to the drowsy hall of Somnus (Sleep) [Hypnos], and bid him send a dream of Ceyx drowned to break the tidings to [his wife] Alcyone.'

Then Iris, in her thousand hues enrobed traced through the sky her arching bow and reached the cloud-hid palace of the drowsy king. Near the Cimmerii a cavern lies deep in the hollow of a mountainside, the home and sanctuary of lazy Somnus [Hypnos] ... There Iris entered, brushing the Somnia (Dreams) [Oneiro] aside, and the bright sudden radiance of her robe lit up the hallowed place; slowly the god his heavy eyelids raised, and sinking back time after time, his languid drooping head nodding upon his chest, at last he shook himself out of himself, and leaning up he recognized her and asked why she came, and she replied : 'Somnus [Hypnos], quietest of the gods, Somnus, peace of all the world, balm of the soul, who drives care away, who gives ease to weary limbs after the hard day's toil and strength renewed to meet the morrow's tasks, bid now thy Somnia (Dreams), whose perfect mimicry matches the truth, in Ceyx's likeness formed appear in Trachis to Alcyone and feign the shipwreck and her dear love drowned. So Juno [Hera] orders.'

Then, her task performed, Iris departed, for she could no more endure the power of Somnus [Hypnos], as drowsiness stole seeping through her frame, and fled away back o'er the arching rainbow as she came ... The old god chose Morpheus to undertake Thaumantias' [Iris'] commands.

Statius, Thebaid 10. 80 ff (trans. Mozley) (Roman epic C1st A.D.):

She [Juno-Hera] determines to make the Aonians [Thebans during the War of the Seven], sunk in the timeless bliss of slumber, a prey to death, and bids her own Iris gird herself with her wonted circles, and commits to her all her task. Obedient to command, the bright goddess leaves the pole and wings her way down her long arc to earth [to the halls of Somnus-Hypnos the god of sleep] . . .

Hither from the blue sky came in balanced flight the varicoloured maid [Iris the rainbow]; the forests shine out, and the shady glens smile upon the goddess, and smitten with her zones of radiance the palace starts from its sleep; but he himself, awoken neither by the bright glow nor by the sound or voice of the goddess, lay motionless as ever, till the Thaumantian [Iris] shot at him all her splendours and sank deep into his drowsy vision. Then thus began to speak the golden fashioner of clouds: 'Somnus [Hypnos], gentlest of the gods, Juno [Hera] bids thee bind fast the Sidonian [Theban] leaders and the folk of ruthless Cadmus, who now, puffed up by the issue of fight, are watching in ceaseless vigil the Achaean rampart, and refuse thy sway. Grant so solemn a request--rarely is this opportunity vouchsafed, to win the favour of Jove [Zeus] with Juno [Hera] on thy side.'

She spoke, and with her hand beat upon his languid breast, and charged him again and yet again, lest her message be lost. He with his own nodding visage nods assent to the goddess' command; o'er-

weighted with the caverns' gloom Iris goes forth, and tricks out her beams, made dim by showers of rain.

Nonnus, Dionysiaca 31. 103 ff (trans. Rouse) (Greek epic C5th A.D.):

Hera made her w ay brooding to the waters of Khremetes [Chremetes, a river of North Africa] in the west ... and she sought out the wife of jealous Zephyros (West-Wind), Iris (Rainbow), the messenger of Zeus when he is in a hurry--for she wished to send her swift as the wind from heaven with a message for shadowy Hypnos (Hypnus, Sleep). She called Iris then, and coaxed her with friendly words: 'Iris, goldenwing bride of plantnourishing Zephyros, happy mother of Eros (Love) [i.e. Pothos]! Hasten with stormshod foot to the home of gloomy Hypnos in the west. Seek also about seagirt Lemnos, and if you find him tell him to charm the eyes of Zeus uncharmable for one day, that I may help the Indians. But change your shape, take the ugly form of Hypnos' mother the blackgirdled goddess Nyx (Night); take a false name and become darkness ... Promise him Pasithea for his bride, and let him do my need from desire of her beauty. I need not tell you that one lovesick will do anything for hope.'

At these words, Iris goldenwing flew away peering through the air ... seeking the wandering track of vagrant Hypnos (Sleep). She found him on the slopes of nuptial Orkhomenos (Orchomenus) ... Then Iris changed her shape, and all unseen she put on the look of dark Nyx unrecognisable. She came near to Hypnos, weaving guile; and in his mother's guise uttered her deceitful speech in cajoling whispers ... Iris begged him to fasten Kronion with slumber for the course of one day only ... Then goddess Iris returned flying at speed and hastened to deliver her welcome message to her queen.

Nonnus, Dionysiaca 20. 188 ff:

Dionysos, did not escape the jealousy of trick-stitching Hera. Still resentful of your divine birth, she sent her messenger Iris on an evil errand, mingling treacherous persuasion with craft, to bewitch you and deceive your mind; and she gave her an impious poleaxe, that she might hand it to the king of Arabia, Lykourgos (Lycurgus), Dryas' son. The goddess made no delay. She assumed a false pretended shape of Ares, and borrowed a face like his. She threw off her embroidered saffron robes, and put on her head a helmet with nodding plume, donned a delusive corselet, as the mother of battle, a corselet stained with blood, and sent froth from her grim countenance, like a man, battlestirring menaces, all delusion. Then with fluent speech she mimicked the voice of Enyalios [Ares]: 'My son, scion of invincible Ares [and persuades Lykourgos to attack Dionysos] . . .'

So he spoke, and goldenwing Iris divine smiled to hear; then went her way, paddling in the false shape of a falcon ... And Iris, by Hera's command, put the winged shoe on her feet, and holding a rod like Hermes the messenger of Zeus, flew up to warn of what was coming. To Bakkhos (Bacchus) in corselet of bronze she spoke deceitful words: 'Brother, son of Zeus Allwise, put war aside, and celebrate your rites with Lykourgos, a willing host . . .'

So she cajoled him, and the shoes carried her high into the air.

Ovid, Metamorphoses 14. 829 (trans. Melville) (Roman epic C1st B.C. to C1st A.D.):

Hersilie (Hersilia), his [Romulus the King of Rome's] consort, mourned his loss, and royal Juno [Hera] bade Iris descend her rainbow and exhort the widowed queen [to visit the grove of her apotheosed husband, the god Quirinus] ... Iris obeyed and gliding down to earth along her many-coloured bow addressed Hersilie in the words prescribed; and she in awe and reverence would hardly raise her eyes. 'Goddess,' she answered, 'who thou art I cannot well surmise, but clear it is thou art a goddess.' . . .

Quickly she reached the hill of Romulus with Thaumantea [Iris]. There a star from heaven dropped gliding to the ground and by its glow set the queen's hair ablaze, and with the star Hersilie ascended to the sky.

Statius, Thebaid 12. 138 ff (trans. Mozley) (Roman epic C1st A.D.):

Iris [sent by Juno-Hera] is bidden cherish the dead bodies [of the Argives who died at Thebes forbidden burial by Kreon (Creon)] of the princes, and laves their decaying limbs with mysterious dews and ambrosial juices, that they may resist the longer and await the pure, nor perish before the flames have seized them.

Messenger of Zeus

Just as Iris is a messenger for Hera, Iris also serves Zeus, sending the winged-one to the halls of other godds.

Valerius Flaccus, Argonautica 4. 6 ff (trans. Mozley) (Roman epic C1st A.D.):

He [Jupiter-Zeus] moved by the goddesses' [Diana-Artemis and Latona-Leto's] tears and Phoebus' [Apollon's] high renown sends down swift Iris on her rosy cloud [to give Herakles permission to release Prometheus from his bonds]. 'Go,' he says, 'let Alcides [Herakles] ... rescue the Titan [Prometheus] from the dreadful Bird.'

Fast flies the goddess and bids the hero quickly perform his sire's commands, and pours the glad message into his eager ears.

Nonnus, Dionysiaca 13. 1 ff (trans. Rouse) (Greek epic C5th A.D.):

Father Zeus sent Iris to the divine halls of Rheia, to inform wakethefray Dionysos, that he must drive out of Asia with his avenging thyrsus the proud race of Indians untaught of justice: he was to sweep from the sea the horned son of a river, Deriades the king, and teach all nations the sacred dances of the vigil and the purple fruit of vintage.

She paddled her way with windswift beat of wings, and entered the echoing den of stabled lions. Noisless her step she stayed, in silence voiceless pressed her lips, a slave before the forest queen. She stood bowing low, and bent down her head to kiss Rheia's feet with suppliant lips. Rheia unsmiling beckoned, and the Korybantes (Corybantes) served her beside the bowl of the divine table. Wondering she drank a sop of the newfound wine, delighted and excited; then with heavy head the spirit told the will of Zeus to the son of Zeus: 'O mighty Dionysos! Your father bids you destroy the race of Indians, untaught of piety. Come, lift the thyrsus of battle in your hands, and earnheaven by your deeds. For the immortal court of Zeus will not receive you without hard work, and the Horai (Horae, Seasons) will not open the gates of Olympos to you unless you have struggled for the prize. Hermeias (Hermes) hardly could win his way to heaven, and only when he had killed with his rod Argos the cowherd, sparkling with eyes from his feet to the hair of his head, and when he had set Ares free from prison [captured in a jar by the Aloidai (Aloadae)]. Apollon mastered Delphyne [Python], and then he came to live in the sky. Even your own father, chief of the Blessed, Zeus Lord in the Highest, did not rise to heaven without hard work, he the sovereign of the stars: first he must bind fast those threateners of Olympos, the Titanes, and hide them deep in the pit of Tartaros. You also do your work, after Apollon, after Hermaon (Hermes), and your prize for your labours will be a home in your father's heaven.'

With these words the goddess returned to Olympos.

Trojan War

During the Trojan War, Iris was called on at several times to carry messages on and off the battlefields, as well as to support the godds. While there are many examples in the *Illiad*, here are a few that stand out for me in terms of showing Iris as not only a messenger, but also a faithful servant and a powerful being in her own right.

To the Trojans, in an image they could recognize:

Homer, Iliad 2. 786 ff (trans. Lattimore) (Greek epic C8th B.C.):

Now to the Trojans came as messenger wind-footed Iris, in her speed, with the dark message from Zeus of the aigis. These were holding assembly standing close at hand swift-running Iris spoke to them, and likened her voice to that of the son of Priamos (Priam), Polites ... In this man's likeness Iris the swift-running spoke to them: 'Old sir, dear to you forever are words beyond number as once, when there was peace; but now stintless war has arisen. In my time I have gone into many battles among men, yet never have I seen a host like this, not one so numerous. These look terribly like leaves, or the sands of the sea-shore, as they advance across the plain to fight by the city. Hektor (Hector), on you beyond all I urge this, to do as I tell you: all about the great city of Priamos are many companions, but multitudinous is the speech of the scattered nations: let each man who is their leader give orders to these men, and let each set his citizens in order, and lead them.'

She spoke, nor did Hektor fail to mark the word of the goddess.

In support of Aphrodite:

Homer, Iliad 5. 352 ff:

The goddess [Aphrodite] departed in pain [from the Trojan battlefield], hurt badly [by Diomedes], and Iris wind-footed took her by the hand and led her away from the battle, her lovely skin blood-darkened, wounded and suffering ... She mounted the chariot and beside her entering Iris gathered the reins up and whipped them into a run, and they winged their way unreluctant. Now as they came to sheer Olympos, the place of the immortals, there swift Iris the wind-footed reined in her horses and slipped them from the yoke and threw fodder immortal before them.

To Hera and Athena:

Homer, Iliad 8. 397 ff:

[Hera and Athena depart for Troy, defying the commands of Zeus:] But Zeus father, watching from Ida, was angered terribly and stirred Iris of the golden wings to run with his message: 'Go forth, Iris the swift, turn them back again, let them not reach me, since we would close in fighting thus that would be unseemly. For I will say this straight out, and it will be a thing accomplished: [He gives her his message.]'

He spoke, and Iris, storm-footed, rose with his message and took her way from the peaks of Ida to tall Olympos, and at the utmost gates of many-folded Olympos, met and stayed them [Athene and Hera from departing for Troy against the express order of Zeus], and spoke the word that Zeus had given her: 'Where so furious? How can your hearts so storm within you? The son of Kronos (Cronus) will not let you stand by the Argives. Since Zeus has uttered this threat and will make it a thing accomplished: [she repeats message verbatim] ... Yes, you [Athene], bold brazen wench, are audacious indeed, if truly you dare lift up your gigantic spear in the face of you father. [She then relays the warning from Zeus.] ... '

So Iris the swift-footed spoke and went away from them.

Message to Poseidon:
Homer, Iliad 15. 145 ff:

[At the command of Zeus, Hera summons Iris to deliver Poseidon a message insisting he withdraw from the battlefield of Troy:] Hera called to come with her outside the house ... [Apollon and] Iris, who is the messenger among the immortal gods, and spoke to them and addressed them in winged words: 'Zeus wishes both of you to go to him with all speed, at Ida; but when you have come there and looked upon Zeus' countenance, then you must do whatever he urges you, and his orders.'

... They in a flash of speed winged their way onward. They came to Ida ... These two came into the presence of Zeus the cloud-gatherer and stood, nor was his heart angry when he looked upon them, seeing they had promptly obeyed the message of his dear lady. He spoke to Iris first of the two, and addressed her in winged words: 'Go on your way now, swift Iris, to the lord Poseidon, and give him all this message nor be a false messenger. Tell him ... [He relates a message.]'

He spoke, and swift wind-footed Iris did not disobey him but went along the hills of Ida to sacred Ilion. As those times when out of the clouds the snow or the hail whirls cold beneath the blast of the north wind born in the bright air, so rapidly in her eagerness winged Iris, the swift one, and stood beside the famed shaker of the earth and spoke to him: 'I have a certain message for you, dark-haired, earth-encircler, and came here to bring it to you from Zeus of the aegis. His order is that ... [She repeats verbatim the message from Zeus.].'

Then deeply vexed the famed shaker of the earth spoke to her ... [Poseidon complains about Zeus' order.] Then in turn swift wind-footed Iris answered him: 'Am I them to carry, o dark-haired earth encircler, this word, which is strong and steep, back to Zeus from you? Or will you change a little? The hearts of the great can be changed. You know the Erinnyes (Furies), how they forever side with the elder.'

Then in turn the shaker of the earth Poseidon spoke to her: 'Now this, divine Iris, was a word quite properly spoken. It is a fine thing when a messenger is conscious of justice.'

To Achilles:

Homer, Iliad 18. 167 ff:

Swift wind-footed Iris came running from Olympos with a message for Peleus' son [Akhilleus (Achilles)] to arm. She came secretly from Zeus and the other gods, since it was Hera who sent her. She came and stood close to him and addressed him in winged words: '[She relays Hera's message.] . . .'

Then in turn Akhilleus of the swift feet answered her: 'Divine Iris, what god sent you to me with a message?'

Then in turn swift wind-footed Iris spoke to him: 'Hera sent me, the honoured wife of Zeus, but the son of Kronos, who sits on high, does not know this, nor any other immortal, of all those who dwell by the snows of Olympos.'

Serving Zeus:

Homer, Iliad 24. 77 ff:

[Zeus addresses Hera:] 'It would be better if one of the gods would summon Thetis here to my presence . . .'

He spoke, and Iris storm-footed sprang away with the message, and at a point between Samos and Imbros of the high cliffs plunged in the *dark water, and the sea crashed moaning about her. She plummeted to the sea floor like a lead weight ... She found Thetis inside the hollow of her cave ... Iris the swift-foot came close beside her and spoke to her: 'Rise, Thetis. Zeus whose purposes are infinite calls you.' ...*

She [Thetis then] went on her way [to Olympos], and in front of her rapid wind-footed Iris guided her, and the wave of the water opened about them. They stepped out on dry land and swept to the sky.

Message to Menelaus:

Stasinus of Cyprus or Hegesias of Aegina, Cypria Fragment 1 (from Proclus, Chrestomanthia) (trans. Evelyn-White) (Greek epic C8th or 7th B.C.):

Iris informs Menelaos (Menelaus) of what has happened at his home [i.e. that Paris has abducted Helene].

With all of this remaining text, it can be easy to see that Iris is the connection point, the transition between, and the instigator of transition. This energy is often what I find in my work with Her, as She is more than an image or a servant; She is the one whose actions cause things to happen. Things that need to happen.

Chapter 3

Symbols & Offerings

Ἶρις
Iris
Sweet One, Dear One
Goddess of Rainbow and the Connection Between
I call to you
I call to the colored arc of your travels
To the wondrous song of your wings
To the beauty of your service
And the sharpness of your messages

Iris, servant to the godds
Keeper of messages and mysteries
Holder of sacred pitchers
And sacred promises

Rainbow mystery
Quietly gliding from the heavens
To the underworld
I call on you for your wisdom
And I follow you to the places
Only you can go

May my heart be in service to others
May my heart be in service to myself
May the colors of my curiosity
Always lead me to perfect knowing
And well-thought-out action

Goddess of Rainbow

Messenger of the Godds
Connection and movement
Action and presentation

May I recognize you when you arrive
Dressed in a message that only i can recognize
And hear when I am ready to hear it

I will sing the song of your presence
And follow the arc of your journeys
To there and back again
To here and back again

Blessed Iris
Blessed one
Daughter of sea and cloud
Holy one
In your colors I know meaning
In your wings I am carried home

Hail Iris
Hail Rainbow

-- Irisanya Moon

While it is clear there were groups that worshipped Iris in ancient times, their practices did not get recorded the same way the practices of Aphrodite or other godds were. Iris is often depicted as having golden wings, carrying a kerykelon (a herald's rod) and an oinochoe (a water pitcher). The rod signified Her role as a herald, and the pitcher often contained nectar for others to drink. In some texts, She is said to have carried a caduceus (a winged staff). Some sources note that the liquid is something needed to talk to spirits. Other texts note that Delians offered cakes, made of wheat, honey and dried figs to Iris.

Common Correspondences

Colors: All

Element: Air

Plants: Iris

Stones: Rainbow quartz, Moonstone, Rainbow moonstone, Opal, Rainbow obsidian.

Incense: Iris, Violet, Lavender, Myrrh, Frankincense.

Symbols: Rainbows, Golden/white wings, Caduceus, Pitcher of water, Clouds, Sun/sunlight.

Offerings: Water, Wine, Honey, Wheat, Figs, Cakes or cookies, Irises, Feathers, Prisms.

According to some sources, Iris led the souls of dead women to the Elysian Fields. And Greeks planted purple irises on the graves of women.

Offering of water were also given to Iris by farmers who gave it in hope it could call again from the clouds to water crops.

Chapter 4

Messenger of the Gods

While Iris does not appear to have a cult (or following), She comes up in a number of stories of the larger Greek godds. She serves Zeus in many stories, helping to pass on messages to godds in need of help or guidance. Iris also serves Achilles, helping to bring winds to his aid. But service can be a tricky commitment. While we may want to serve, I encourage service that is in alignment with values and honoring of reciprocity.

Perhaps one does not go into service to get something in return, but you also can not be in service if you are not serving yourself in some way. To me, Iris has been a great teacher of this conversation. After all, when serving others, I may have skills and abilities that are useful, but that does not mean that I always have to be the one to step forward.

Service to the Godds

One of the lingering pieces of patriarchal society and Christian practices is the idea of subservience. Because the godds or God is 'higher' than others, this means service is in supplication, as though living is the gift and acts of service are gratitude for that gift. Iris does show that She will always serve the godds, but even as you begin to deepen into Her stories, you will see that She is not always bearing the message in the way it was originally stated. Sometimes, She arrives in the image of someone from whom the person can more easily hear the message.

In my practice of Witchcraft, I am a priestess and I serve my community through teaching, ritual planning, priestessing, and spiritual counseling/mentoring. I also serve the godds when they ask me to serve. I have been asked to pass on messages and I have been asked to connect with certain people. Sometimes,

I don't even know I've been asked. I may just find myself in a certain conversation and then I realize why I'm there. My point in this section is that Iris is a godd to certainly build a relationship with, but She can also be a deity that offers the opportunity to better connect and serve other godds.

Service to the Self

One of the things I wish we knew about Iris was how She felt about Her role. I imagine that She was given the role and not really given a choice, but with so much we know about other Greek godds and their internal conflicts, it's a shame Iris doesn't have the same details (at least that I could find).

I can imagine always being the messenger and the errand-runner may have been tiresome at first. Not only do you see what the godds ask and ask for again and again, but you also would be the one carrying the message and likely getting the anger or ire of the recipient. It's like Iris is the face of the company, but not the one who makes the decisions. I bring this up because if Iris teaches us of service to the godds, I don't feel it's blind service, even if we don't see Her get upset or annoyed by Her role. She is not human. You are.

If there's anything I have learned time and time again in my priestessing and witchcraft work, it's that I also have to serve myself. I need to set aside time for nourishing practices and my own interests. When I don't, I become angry and resentful of the things I agree to do, even if I really want to do them. Service to yourself is necessary for sustainability in any relationship. You need to be able to take care of your own needs first, which will then allow you to decide if you want to take on more tasks from others.

I do not believe in wringing myself out to serve the godds. I believe they want me to be happy. I believe they want me to delight in my own life too. A tired and burnout priestess is not a very effective servant, after all.

Practice: Balancing Service

To make sure you honor yourself in the way you serve the godds and yourself, and especially with Iris in mind, balance is vital. To be clear, I don't feel balance is a static practice. It is a practice of continuously adjusting to see what works in a particular moment or movement. When you are called to serve in some capacity, I offer the practice of discernment.

- Is this something I want to do?
- Is this something I have time to do?
- Is this something I have resources to do?

Because these questions take time to consider, I would highly recommend you take at least 24 hours to think on any request of your service. I know in this world of instant answers, it might seem strange to ask for time, but it will help you truly hear the answer that's right for you. You can even call on Iris to help you with your decision-making. You can ask if She can talk to the godds about your decision or if She has any advice for you.

Taking time will allow you to make the best decision for you and for the state you are in at the moment. Nothing requires your immediate attention. And if it does require your immediate attention, check in with yourself about how YOU feel about the service, not whether it will be good for another person. Make sure it's good for you first.

No matter what you say and what you offer, make sure to balance it with time for yourself. I often will count how many hours I am teaching or priestessing and try to give myself that many hours of no-commitment free time. It doesn't always work out perfectly, but the more I balance the two, the more I enjoy both.

Chapter 5

Traveling the Rainbow – A Magickal Practice

When working with Iris, there are a number of ways to approach Her mystery. You might cultivate a personal practice or be more attuned to messages from the godds or you might travel the rainbow that arrives with Her. I personally find that looking at nature as a guide is the most authentic way to approach magick. While we might focus on a deity or a being, we can look to the world around us to inform our own personal work.

In this section, I would also offer that even though many of these practices focus on you, they can also be applied to the larger work and your interests. For example, you might look at these practices as ways to gain insight into activism, into your community, or into your ancestors. I offer these practices as possibilities, not prescriptions. She offers magick in the way rainbows form, seemingly from nothing, but truly from the perfect alignment of conditions.

If we extend the metaphor into your presence at this time right now, you have placed yourself in the perfect position to learn from Iris, to grow, and to navigate storms as gifts of beauty.

How Rainbows are Formed

The more I started to see rainbows, the more I began to see how certain conditions needed to be present in order for things to happen.

- Rain
- Sunlight
- Placement of the viewer

Where I live in Northern California in the United States, rainbows often come in the winter time, when the rains come. While this land is lucky to be green and lush during typically colder months in the Northern Hemisphere, this is also a time when the rains do not always come as much as they need to nourish the land before the long dry times.

I will begin to see rainbows in November during typically rainy seasons. While there might only be one rain or a few hours of rain, since the sun is still in the sky for a while, it sets up the perfect time for rainbows. Yes, rain or water is necessary. But there also needs to be sunlight. In a place where microclimates occur, this is a more frequent event. However, it does not always mean you will or can see a rainbow.

Where you are positioned in the wind also determines whether you see the gift of the many-colored bow. Sunlight needs to strike a raindrop or many raindrops in order to be reflected away from the drop. The rest of the light will get refracted by the raindrop by traveling through the water. When this happens, the white light splits into many colors -- red, orange, yellow, green, blue, indigo, and violet.

From there, more needs to happen to create a visible rainbow. The different colors are then reflected behind the raindrop at the proper angle to create a rainbow (if it does not happen at a precise angle, you will not see a rainbow) and then refracted again, this time more quickly since it has less distance to travel. From there, the light is much more vibrant and any white light is split out more, causing the large lines of colors in the sky.

Some rainbows will last a long time due to the perfect conditions. While other rainbows might only appear for a few moments or only in sections. When conditions are perfect, there are large arcs of rainbows that travel across the sky, following the shape of the earth.

So many steps happen to conjure the magick of water and light. And from there, Iris travels and is seen carrying messages.

Some say She travels in forms that people can recognize. I believe the rainbow is one of those forms. It is instantly recognizable, but also not an everyday event. To further your relationship with Iris and Her magick, I offer a seven part or day or whenever-you-like practice that follows the many steps that it takes to make a rainbow. The ways you might take to shine as brightly too. While it makes sense to the logical brain to follow things in order, if you are not called to do so, you do not have to go step by step. Or you might try and see what arrives for you.

RED: Sunlight + Rain

Perfect conditions are impossible, it seems. So, let's begin in the seemingly impossible. We're taught from a young age that things can only be bad or good. You can only be sad or happy. But as we grow older, we recognize this is only not true, but it limits the ways in which we can experience the world.

Move Your Body

I invite you to begin your practice in the place that you are. A place that likely includes both light and raindrops. Both beauty and nuisance. Or beyond binary thinking. Or something that includes three or more qualities in your life.

Name those qualities. Bring them into the place you are. Allow them to be seen and witnessed and known for how they already belong to the story you're creating and the messages you're making with each breath in your life. With each song. With each sigh. With each wail.

I invite you to begin in sacred and scared space. I describe this as the place of being as you are, complicated and true. We are never simply one thing at a time. We are many things, many experiences, many reactions, and many histories. To embody this in the present, you will need:

- Music that makes you feel good.

- Music that makes you feel less than what you want to be.
- Music that brings a smile to your face.
- Music that makes you cry.

In any way that works for you, bring yourself to a space that is quiet and still. A place where you won't be interrupted and where you can feel free. If you do not have a private space, you can do this practice in your head as well. Your body does not need to move at all. Follow the energy of what is happening and you will complete the work you need to complete.

I invite you to create a playlist or have these songs readily available. Move from song to song, really tapping into experiences in your life that have pushed you through different emotional landscapes. Picture where you were, what you were doing, who was there, what you felt, and how you made it through.

And when I offer the idea of making it through, this doesn't necessarily mean successfully. Some bad days are just days you need to complete. They might not be fixable or offer life-changing growth. They might just be a part of the weather. And like the weather, they shift again. No matter what you do.

If your body feels good, I invite you to move along with these landscapes of song. With the messages of lyrics that resonate or melodies that speak to you. Let yourself go into these places without trying to fix or change or gain insight. Move in your mind, if you like. Picturing or sensing into what it feels like to interact in these spaces. Trust the wisdom of your body and the knowing of your experience. All have a place and all have a gift to offer. If you can, the more you listen, let go of attachment to anything that might come or arrive. Just be in the moment. Allow your body and mind to guide you and hold you and know you as you are.

Once you have moved or engaged as much as you like, sit or lay down on the ground (if you aren't already). And just be still. Let the clouds of your awareness settle. Know that you hold all of the complexities of rain and sun. You hold storms and clearing.

Touch your heart or your belly or another part of you that feels like home. Thank your body for holding all of it, even when you didn't want to. Especially when you didn't want to. All of these moments are precious moments. They are precious opportunities to move from what you're supposed to be and what you're supposed to do. To just be a perfect moment. No matter what.

- Perhaps you didn't know you could hold grief in one hand and love in the other.
- Perhaps you didn't realize you could be ecstatic and angry.
- Perhaps you didn't understand that you are multiple experiences, unfolding.

Hold yourself in this understanding. In this possibility. Anchor this in your body as a reminder that all can be perfect in the presence of seemingly contradictory emotions. There is no right way to be with yourself. Find a part of you and hold it like you might hold a young child. Let it know how perfect it is. Offer it the healing words or touch that it needs to truly feel your willingness to be in the rain and the sun with it.

Once you are done, perhaps get out a journal to write down anything that you learned or realized in this experience. Come back to this practice as often as you like. As often as you need to come back to yourself.

ORANGE: Reflection

While mirror work can be some of the most confronting work we can do, it can also be some of the most rewarding. For this practice, you will need a mirror that allows you to see your whole face. If you have a full-length mirror, even better. This is a practice that can be intense for some, so I invite you to do this at a time when you can be alone afterward. Or at a time when you can be with someone who supports you well and who will be willing to comfort any rough edges that might linger.

Mirror Work

In a place that is safe and away from others, I invite you to look into the mirror. I invite you to travel the space of your skin and feel the way you are shaped -- perfectly and precisely. Travel the length of your body to understand what you are and who you might be in the world now.

Watch the way your hand moves on your body and see the stories you tell. Talk to yourself about what you feel and what you have to say, making sure to look at yourself in the mirror as you do. What are the words you use? What are the messages you send to yourself? Are there things that surprise you? Are there things that anger you?

I invite you to offer yourself the gift of honesty. Do not censor what you say because you feel you shouldn't say it. This is a practice of truly seeing as the sunlight travels the edges of a raindrop, the light that isn't broken up, but rather it lingers, waiting for its turn to break into color. As you send messages to yourself, messages you may have said over and over again, you might notice you want to reassure yourself. You might begin to feel the soft stretch of movement over water. If you find you tear up or cry, feel that water as the gift of honoring the reflection as it is right now. As you are right now.

Allow and be present for all of it. If you are moved to change the messages, do so. Go back to those places on your body to say something different, something softer. Something more specific. What do you love about this skin? What do you know about this heart? What do you know about this body's shape? How do you reflect back to yourself? How might you reflect something new?

Find a phrase that feels like a truer message to gift to yourself. Look in the mirror. Look in your eyes and repeat it again and again until the words do not sound like words anymore. Trace the words on your skin. Trace the words on the mirror. Look in your eyes and see what reflects back now. To care for yourself after this practice, I encourage you to:

- Keep your experience to yourself for a while.
- Write down what you noticed and the message you want to repeat.
- Repeat that message to yourself every time you are in front of a mirror or reflective surface.
- Take a soothing bath or shower to continue to love on your body.
- Watch your dreams for messages from Iris.
- Ask Iris to bless your work.

You might find you need more water or more food to help you feel grounded. You might find you need a few days to come back to your body. You might also find you feel more in tune with your body. You might feel something completely different. If you notice any rough edges, again, it can help to talk to a close friend about what you might need or to be held by someone who makes you feel safe. And if you can, dance in the raindrops. Find a body of water to see your reflection in. Continue to look at all you are.

YELLOW: Refraction

If your heart is broken, make art with the pieces.
-- Shane Koyczan

For this practice, I invite you to gather up any art supplies that call to you. This might be as simple as a piece of paper and pen or you might have colorful markers and pencils. If you can, find a large piece of paper that can hold a lot of space for the threads of your life. You can also use a large piece of cardboard or attach smaller pieces together to create a large working space. You might want to gather pictures from your childhood here. Pictures you can use in the art.

In the process of refraction, light is split into different colors. And only by being broken up can beauty emerge. It's a lovely metaphor for life. But how do we hold brokenness when the world wants us to be perfectly put back together? Art is often the way.

You may have heard of vision boards and dream boards as ways to create a vision for moving forward. This is a great practice too and one that you could certainly use to create a new vision for moving ahead into the rainbow brilliance. Or, you can start with the broken pieces and allow them to inform what happens next.

Our lives are made up of separate points and interactions. Our lives have people and places that have informed our decisions and our indecision. Sometimes, we want to just move on. Sometimes, we want to forget. But we do not forget. Because at certain moments, when the light moves a certain way, our 'togetherness' can be broken up into all of the pieces. And we see it all. There are two ways to work on the first round of refraction.

- Collage of What You Decided
- Map of What Happened to You

You can choose one or the other or both. Or you might be inspired by either of these practices to do something that feels more in alignment with your life's pieces.

Collage of What You Decided

Before you begin to collage, make a list of seven things where you made a decision that changed everything. These might be decisions to move to certain places or to take on certain jobs or responsibilities. Just make sure this is a list of things that you chose.

These are points at which you were in your power and you were acting from your values. Once you have those points, begin to seek out pictures or images or words from magazines or other materials that represent those moments. Try not to think too hard about it. Try not to get too focused on something being right. If something brings up a feeling, go with that image or images.

Continue to collect images until you have every point on your list covered. (For those without collage materials, drawings are fine. For those without a desire to collage, writing small descriptions is fine.) With these images and words, begin to place them on the large piece of paper or cardboard you collected. Do not worry about order or appearance. Follow your heart to see where things might go, where they fit. Forget about artistic expression and balance. Just place things where they need to be as you see it today.

If you wrote, then you might take the sentences and print them out and place them in a new order on a page of paper. Or you might use your word processing program's copy and paste to move things around. Again, don't think too hard. Refraction happens as it does.

Once everything is in place. Stop. Close your eyes. After a moment, open your eyes again to see what has emerged. (This practice is even better in a group that offers what they see, without trying to explain the meaning.) What are the images? What are the shapes? How do things fit together? When everything is broken up and put back together, what happens then? Do meanings change? Do feelings change? What happens when you actively engage with refraction and how your decisions came together?

After journaling or sharing reflections, take a moment to thank the pieces of your life that led to this moment. To the points where you broke off from what others thought of you and chose yourself first.

Map of What Happened to You

While bringing together the pieces of decisions can seem to be the more empowering practice, it is also powerful to bring together the pieces where you were not in control. Those pieces too have a story to show and to tell you. You were given messages and when you were young, you took those messages on. You may not have understood them or wanted them. You may not have realized those messages were wrong or hurtful. You took them on because you didn't know differently.

This practice is about presencing those messages and the things that happened to you. Before beginning, I want to make it very clear: you don't have to give up your deepest, darkest secrets here. You can bring out only the things you want to see again or that you feel safe to explore again. If you have any hesitation at any point, stop. If your emotions begin to feel too big, stop. While we're often told that feeling pain is how we get through things, it is also unnecessary to hurt ourselves or perpetuate the hurt of the past. If you're not sure about this practice, skip it. Or only choose one message or experience that you can handle right now.

If you feel like you can navigate this practice, I invite you to find a time or a point in your life when you were given a message. Take that message and make a representation of it. It could be the words or it could be a representation of the feeling it evoked.

Place that on the piece of paper. Along the outside of the image, place arrows or lines outward. These lines will connect to where that message came from. People. Places. Situations. Circumstances. What led to that messaging? The patriarchy? Your parents? Your teachers? Your friends?

Figure out where things came from. Map it out. Get as detailed as you like. Find out the source of your personal refraction. Where did you split off from your internal messaging? Where did you get pushed into a position of breaking up into different pieces?

Because this is the place where refraction only starts to form a rainbow, there may be moments of beauty in knowing that you are beyond these points. Or you might break the light into pieces of recognising these messages as still being a part of you.

No matter what, breathe and feel what you feel. If breathing isn't right for this moment, move your body in a way that feels right and freeing. Allow any of this experience to move through your present being. And take that piece of paper or whatever you have created (for both of these exercises) and place it in water. Let it set outside in the sunshine to be transformed.

GREEN: Splitting

Because different colors of light move at different speeds, our eyes perceive them differently. While one might move quickly and show up one way, another moves slowly and we see another color. This message of movement and perception also incorporates the idea that we might have all that we need inside of ourselves. It might be that it's more of some things moving at different speeds before they can be seen and realized and integrated into everyday life.

Think about a time when you were given a message by someone else, a message or piece of advice you didn't take in. While you may not have realized it at that point, you were missing a vital moment. However, you might also notice that later on, when someone else said the same thing, it made sense. You were able to take it in. It doesn't mean you were doing anything wrong by missing things in the first place. I would offer this just means things arrive at the speed they're meant to arrive.

Spells and Time

To work with this idea of colors splitting and being seen for their radiance because they move at different speeds, I invite you to work on two spells at the same time. If you haven't done this before, no worries. We're going to make them simple. (And if you have done this before, you can make things as complicated as you like, though I encourage simplicity this time.)

Find two things in your life that you want to bring info form and reality. This might be something like a new job or a better partnership or a certain amount of money. Come up with two things that are concrete and that you don't already have. I would also say that these should not be emergent things. We're going to work with time a bit to see how we might bend it and how it might bend our expectations.

Find two places in your room or home or other location where you can work each spell on an altar. I find altars to be a very simple and personalized way to work magick, and they can be hidden if you are a practitioner who is not necessarily out in the open. One space should be in constant shadow and one space should be in constant light. Think about a closet and a windowsill. In each of these spaces, create an altar to something you want. It could include an image of what you want or a written explanation or intention. You might choose a colored candle for each altar, depending on what you feel the energy is for that spell. And I encourage you to be intuitive about this, rather than trying to find the 'perfect' way to do this.

Spend 30 days focusing on each of these altars. This might mean spending a few minutes a day thinking about your intention or goal. Bring up the emotions and the experiences associated with the goal. Close your eyes and try to see yourself with these items in your life. Look out for messages in your world about what you need to do to bring that into your life. It can be helpful to focus on one in the morning and one at night.

When I'm focusing on a goal or spell, I might wake up in the morning, go to my altar, think on this magickal working, and then move out in the world looking for signs.

- What songs do I hear?
- What messages do people give me?

- What does my horoscope say?
- How does my body feel?
- What (literal) signs do I see? e.g., billboards, store announcements, etc.
- What surprising things happen?
- What breaks?
- What comes into my life during this time?
- Do I feel more or less attached to the outcome?

I invite this to be a practice of having openness to messages and to the ways that things arrive in the time they arrive. And at no time do I want you to feel that the goal is to bring these things into your life. They might come -- and great. But this is more a practice of watching to see if there are signs that will help you better understand the best timing. Even if it's not your timing.

Getting Still Enough

Another practice that might help you with the practice of bending in the way the universe works on its own timeline is to learn how to be perfectly present in this moment. Meditation is a great way to do this. But I want to be clear that meditation does not need to look like sitting very still and in a rigid posture. I often meditate in the morning after I wake up, while lying in bed.

Here's a simple way to bring meditation into your life and to bring yourself more into alignment with the possibility that you are already on the right path. To align with the idea that things that are yours are already on their way.

- Find a place where you can be still and safe and alone
- Sit or lay down
- Close your eyes or keep them half closed with a soft gaze
- Take a breath or stretch your body
- Count to 100 at a steady pace
- Open your eyes or widen them to come back to the space

That practice will likely take no more than two minutes, depending on the speed of your counting and the time it takes to get settled. One of the biggest misconceptions about meditation is that it's a practice of getting rid of all thoughts -- but that's not the case. It's about teaching ourselves to be in the present moment and let unnecessary thoughts drift by.

We're going to think. We're going to think about what's happening next, if we're doing something right, if we're good enough, if we should have nachos for our next meal, etc. Even when you count, you might still have other ideas and thoughts. It's okay. But the more you do this practice of getting still and letting thoughts just come in and go out, the more you will be present in the current moment. When you're present in the current moment, not only can you see the signs and hear the messages, but you will also be able to do something about them.

You can also see that things are happening in the time they are meant to happen. No longer will you worry for hours about what you've done in the past or what you might do (or not do) in the future. Practice giving this time back to yourself. Listen to yourself and the way Iris calls to you when you're not racing around to find the next best step.

BLUE: More Reflection

I found it amazing when I learned how rainbows were formed because it started to better reflect (so to speak) the way I experienced my life. Instead of it being a very linear process in which something follows something else in sequence, rainbows arrive when they are reflected, refracted, broken, and then reflected and refracted again.

Even though it doesn't seem fair or easy, life seems to offer this to us. It offers moments of opportunity and learning to really come into ourselves with the movement from one state to another -- much like the alchemical process.

In order to change or shift or arrive in the places we're meant to be, we need to be willing to bend and move in a new way. As we move into the blue practice of reflection, I think of water. I think of the way that water reflects different images at different angles. Sometimes things look broken in the water because of the way light hits it. And sometimes look exactly as they are.

But the truth is that a reflection is never something that reveals the truth of our image. When we look in mirrors, we see a reversed image of ourselves. At no time in our lives will we ever see ourselves head on. Even cameras distort reality. We never really see ourselves. At least not what we look like. However, we can gaze at what we reflect from the inside out.

Water Gazing

While most people think of Iris as the traveler who moves between Olympus and Earth, this is only a part of the story, as you have now learned. Iris is also a being who can travel and does travel to the River Styx. This river that is between the land of the living and the dead is the river that causes fear for many. Crossing over means never coming back. Getting to this place means you need to pay a toll to the ferryman to get you across. It means you need to offer something of value in order to continue your journey. Water carries us from birth and in this mythos, it carries us to death.

What does water have to tell us and reflect back to us in these days when we are alive? I would offer that reflections and being present to all they offer can be a place of knowing.

What you need:

A large bowl
Water
A candle
A dark room

It can also help to have a bowl that is dark in color or one that is silver or gold to add reflection, but it's not necessary. Allow yourself to be in a safe place and it might help to create some sacred space in the way that feels good to you. Ask Iris to travel to these waters with you. Fill the bowl about halfway with water. Light the candle and place it where it can reflect into the water.

When the water stills after you have poured it, sit beside the bowl and soften your gaze. Allow yourself to sink into the water with your mind. If you find you are getting pulling out of the practice, you can hum to yourself or put on instrumental music in the background to keep you from jumping out of the experience. It can also help to gaze at the candle for a few moments and then back to the water.

Allow whatever images arrive to arrive, and allow whatever feelings to be the right things to feel. Let the energy of Iris drape over your shoulders and into your arms and into the water. Allow Her to push you into the place of seeing and knowing. There are messages in the ripples and there are messages in the waiting.

I encourage you to stay in this practice for a while, or until you cannot focus anymore. Once you are done, give thanks to Iris and to any other energies you called in. It can help for you to write out what your impressions were. What did you see? What did you sense? What became clear? What became murkier? This is also helpful when you are curious about a certain question in your life. And you can also use cloud or sky gazing as a complementary practice, as Iris travels across those too. What might you find there if you follow Her path?

Making Sacred Promises

When the godds were taking sacred oaths, Iris was the one who traveled to the River Styx to collect water in Her pitcher. As the godd was making their oath, Iris would pour the water out of the pitcher. And the godd would be bound to their oath.

Making oaths is not a practice to be taken lightly. When you make oaths, you make promises that you are to keep, no matter how they impact other parts of your life. No matter how your life changes between when you make that oath and another moment in time. In some texts, it is said that godds who perjure themselves after drinking of the River Styx to make promises are put to sleep by Iris for an entire year.

I offer that sacred promises are the moments we devote ourselves fully. We are committing to doing something, big or small, in service. And Iris is truly in service to the godds. (Plus, I might point out that by being in service to the godds, She is also in service to Her self and Her purpose.) Are you willing to make sacred promises? Are you willing to take an oath of service to yourself? Or are you ready to promise something else?

While many of these practices have been simpler and seem to invite immediate participation, I would encourage you to slow at this point and think about a promise you want to make in your life. Whether this is to yourself or to someone else, a promise kept is a promise with power. And when you keep a promise, it strengthens your promises in the future. Not only will you have a positive history of promises being kept and people will believe you, but you will also believe in yourself. Take time to listen to yourself about what you need in your life. What might you need to promise yourself?

- I will care for myself first.
- I will not abandon myself again.
- I will prioritize my family.
- I will eat well and move my body
- I will keep within a budget.
- I promise to _____.

You can also make this promise contained within a certain time period. This way, you can evaluate if you've made the right promise. If you can't seem to keep it, perhaps you need to adjust. That's completely okay.

Another practice that I recommend is small promises that you keep each day with yourself, like a daily commitment. You might promise to drink a cup of water when you wake up. Or to get up at a certain time. And the more you do this, the more trust you build in yourself.

If you have come up with a larger promise, you can set aside time to promise this to Iris as well. It's ideal to have a pitcher for this practice, filled with water. You can perform this outside or inside, depending on what you have access to and feel called to. Bring yourself to a grounded state in which you are clear about what you are promising and you have the words clearly in your mind. Recognize that this is something that you will uphold no matter what, even if it's just for a short time.

Repeat your promise aloud or in your mind while holding the pitcher. Feel the energy of your words and your intention flow through the container and into the water. Continue to charge up this water until it feels a little heavier than it did before you started working your magick. Once the pitcher feels full to you, lift it up and offer it to Iris. Move the pitcher down to below the earth and offer it to Styx. When you have made these offerings and presentations, pour the water into the earth or into a drain that will eventually go back to the earth.

Watch the water pour slowly from the pitcher. Your promise is now being held by the godds and it is sacred. It travels into the space of growing and knowing. It moves at the pace of intention. Keep your senses open to the possibility of what might emerge because of this promise.

INDIGO: More Refraction

Another refraction and being bent to reveal more color, more messages, more deep wisdom. Iris can offer you solace here, but also service. Her movements between the worlds are not movements everyone can make.

It is easy to say that these travels are only for the godds, but you have traveled to the great above and the great below in your life. You have been to the happiest day and the worst day. You have been to the places that elate you and places that scare you. You know you can travel there, even if you didn't try to go in that direction. Sometimes, the movement happens. The journey comes to you. You are meant to go where you arrive.

Trance to the Lower World and the Heavens

For those who are not aware, many practices divide the worlds into different landscapes, often called the upper, middle, and lower worlds. In Greek mythology, the Underworld is ruled by Hades, the middle world is the world of humans, and the upper world is the Heavens.

Set aside a long period of time for this trance and after-experience. An hour is a good starting point. In this practice, I encourage you to move with the speed and grace of Iris, between the worlds. Again, it is best to record this practice so you can simply sink into it, but as you begin to understand the process of trance, you can also do this in a way that works best for you.

Make sure you are in a space that is safe and a place where you will not be interrupted. You can choose to lay down or sit or to walk the steps of moving between worlds.

Realize that you can do whatever you want to do in this journey. If the words I use are not the right words, use words and images that are better for you. You are in control and you are able to shift to what is best for your body and mind today.

Allow yourself to settle in the way that serves you best today. This might be the settling that feels like slowing your breathing or shaking your body until you release tension. Or it might be another practice that works best for you.

Drop your awareness down the length of your body to your feet and ankles, allowing them to be as they are today and allowing anything that does not serve to drop, to sink, to fall away.

(wait a few moments)

Notice your awareness float to the space of knees and thighs and pelvic bowl, swirling around in the space between hip bones, allowing them to be as they are today and allowing anything that does not serve to drop, to sink, to fall away.

(wait a few moments)

And then your awareness moves to the space of your digestion and will and center and resting there, allow them to be as they are today and allow anything that does not serve to drop, to sink, to fall away.

(wait a few moments)

Once again, your awareness moves to the space of your lungs and heart, encased in a protective ribcage, allow them to be as they are today and allowing anything that does not serve to drop, to sink, to fall away.

(wait for a few moments)

And your awareness travels the space of shoulders and arms and elbows and wrists and fingers, allowing them to be as they are today and allowing anything that does not serve to drop, to sink, to fall away.

(wait a few moments)

Traveling again to the space of the neck and jawbone and face, around the contours of your eyes and ears, and up to the forehead and top of the head, allowing them to be as they are today and allowing anything that does not serve to drop, to sink, to fall away.

(wait a few moments)

From this space, you can widen your awareness out and long. To the stretches of horizon and across waters, moving to the place of expanse and revelation. Perhaps you notice a path that can take you to Iris again or perhaps She quickly comes to meet you. Allow whatever needs to happen for the two of you to connect.

(wait a few minutes)

Once you feel Iris' presence, I invite you to ask Her if you can travel together. There might be moments where this is something She wants to help you with and sometimes not. Just as we are in choice with our magick, the godds have agency as well.

If She is not willing to travel with you, then spend some time with Her to see what She might have to say to you. Realize this might simply be the right time for you to turn back and return to your body.

If She is willing to travel with you, then I invite you to give gratitude and ask what you need to do to prepare. What might you need to do for your body? Your heart? Your spirit?

Listen deeply. Prepare as you need. Take the time you need.

(wait a few minutes)

The first place that Iris will take you is to the underworld and you travel there in a way that is right for you. What do you notice as you travel together? What happens? What do you feel or sense? What does your body feel like? What does your heart feel like as you move down and down and down and down?

(wait a few moments)

As you see the underworld with your eyes or your mind, you can begin to see the River Styx and the ferryman who waits to take you over. Iris lets you know this is not the way you will go. You are of the living and not of the dead right now.

She shows you what She shows you of the underworld. Allow yourself to experience what She feels is important for you to know today.

(wait a few minutes)

And when you feel ready or Iris gives you a sign, you begin to leave the underworld. You rise up and notice Iris' wings and the rainbow that trails behind. Or you see something else that She wants to show you.

Take notice of the travel now. What does it feel like? What do you feel like? What does your heart feel like? What do you notice?

(wait a few moments)

You might begin to move through clouds and see the outline of Olympus. What does it look like to you? What does it feel like to you to know this is the place of godds too? What is here for you?

Iris takes you to the heavens and the place of godds. You are most likely to see Hera and Zeus, but there might be others who want to see this being that Iris brought. Allow yourself time to be with the godds, even if you don't know their names or recognize their faces. Take in these messages too. Take in this experience too.

(wait a few minutes)

But after a time, you realize you can't be in this space forever. Iris begins to motion that you can now travel back to where you began. She is going to stay with the godds. You can thank Her for Her help. Or you can ask another question or take some other action that feels right to you in this moment.

(wait a few moments)

And then you feel yourself float back down. Down, down, down to the places of your body and the top of your head.

Down, down, down

Down through the space of your forehead, eyes, jaw, and throat.

Down, down, down

Down through the space of arms and collarbone.

Down, down, down

Down through the space of ribcage, heart, and lungs.

Back to your body

Into the space of digestion, will, and power

Back to your body

Into the space between hip bones, your pelvic bowl, and thighs

Back to your body

Back to the space of your knees, calves, and ankles

Back to this moment

Once again, take the care you need to take to come back to your body. It can help to touch your body's edges and it can help to do something that uses another part of your body. You might ask yourself how much money you spent yesterday or how much a certain bill is this month. Take the time you need to come back to the present. You did a lot of traveling. And it might have seemed like minutes or days.

It might be wise to journal about this experience of traveling. And it might be wise to think about how you have traveled between underworld and heavens. What has happened? What did you do well? What might you have learned from Iris in how She travels?

I invite you to practice this traveling as often as once a week. This will allow you to not only continue to feel comfortable with the practice, but also to feel more resilient when things like this happen in your life. As they will.

VIOLET: Dispersion

When you have worked on your personal development and you have worked on relationships with the godds, it can be confusing to know what happens next. I know I've been confused when I have learned a lot and I have grown a lot, but the world around me doesn't really seem all that different. Where are the rainbows? Where are the signs telling me I did something right or the signs that I'm done?

Firstly, you are never done with uncovering places to explore in yourself. I truly believe you are an endless landscape of more light and colors. Which is beautiful and overwhelming, to be sure. I think it becomes most overwhelming and intimidating when it's unclear what happens next. And I can't really answer that for you. Perhaps Iris can. Perhaps you have the answer too.

Integration

The work I have done with Iris has been more important when it comes to integrating my spiritual practices. I used to think integration was some sort of step-by-step process that I just didn't know. But it's far from a clear place. It's turning to inner knowing and resources. It's turning to all that you have, rain and sunlight, position and awareness. It's the act of bringing it all together. Here is what I think I can offer about integration right now:

- **Don't rush to know** - Perhaps you are someone who likes to get to the end or the 'point' of what you're doing. You want to be handed down the knowledge like a download or a well-wrapped gift of clarity. It doesn't always happen like that. Knowledge might be quick, but wisdom takes time. Give yourself permission to know without needing to understand everything. This can look like reviewing your journal daily to see what you wrote and seeing how things land over time.

- **Notice when you use tools** - The best example of integration is the moment when you use a tool you have learned without thinking about it. For example, when you just go and make a sacred promise or you use water to learn about the next best steps for yourself. In these moments, be grateful and remind yourself that this is wisdom and integration too. When these practices are just a part of you now.

- **Give yourself space** - Often after large magickal workings or initiations, participants are given the challenge of resting and not taking on new work. This allows for space for things to settle and to become more integrated. Learn and then rest.

- **Go back as needed** - You may have moments where certain ideas come into your mind and you can't quite remember what you learned. Go back to your journals to remind yourself of the context of the learning and that will help with integration too.

And while you have probably already guessed, taking care of your physical body is essential when you're doing energetic work. Eat foods that nourish you, drink water, and move your body as you can. The more you can support your body in its role as foundation, the more it will support you too.

Embracing Your Brilliance

One of the questions I consider is whether rainbows know how brilliant they are. Do they understand how people admire them? Do they realize how they are photographed and shared around the world? They are seen as signs of hope and faith. Rainbows are harbingers of storms ending and the light returning. A moment when all is well because certain conditions are in place.

How about you? Do you know how brilliant you are? Do you understand how you light up the world with your beauty? If not, it's time to find it and to witness it. I invite you to reach out to a few beloved friends for their input. From their perspective, ask them about your brilliance.

- What are you good at?
- What do they admire about you?
- How have you impacted them?
- What do you not realize about yourself?

You can choose to email these questions to your friend or, if you're willing, you can ask them to talk about it face-to-face or over the phone. If you notice you're a person who is less than eager to take in what others think about you, let this be a moment of courage and pushing against these edges of your experience. What if you are so brilliant to others, but you never hear it?

What if you are inspiring others in ways that you don't realize -- and you could offer even more if only you knew? Once you have collected these responses, it's a good practice to write them down (if they're not ready in print) and keep them somewhere you can read them often. Allow them to be the messages that can inspire you to stop and remember who you are. And if your friends feel inspired, you might offer your insights back, creating intimacy and connection and reciprocity in the practice.

Sending Messages Out into the World
I admit that one of the things that has pushed me in my magickal

work in the world is the knowledge that people feel alone in their struggles (and their joys). There are so many who don't understand the brilliance they are because they're comparing it to someone else's brilliance or measuring stick. And to be clear, I have a lot of these days too. And on those days, I try to be a messenger of love and hope.

What if you could be too? If Iris is in service to the godds, what if you might be in service to your community? What if you might share messages that inspire and remind people of their connection and value? This doesn't have to be complicated at all. And it doesn't have to be costly.

- Text or email people - Make a goal of reaching out to just one person a day and you will make connections often, but not so often that it's draining to you.
- Save things that remind you of them - I have a practice of keeping images and memes I find online for folks I know, folks who will appreciate them.
- Send little notes or gifts - You don't have to buy things, but you could send a little postcard to others or leave a small gift on their doorstep when they're not expecting it. Even a flower you picked from your yard with a note is a perfect way to remind others they are brilliant in your life.
- Share time with others - Make time for those you love and those you care for. It doesn't have to be a lot of time, but a little time shared is a lot of loneliness diminished.
- Remember special events - I also have reminders in my phone and calendar of birthdays and other events, so I can reach out to folks on those days.
- Post positive things on social media - Since you don't have contact information for everyone in the world, I like to post things on my social media accounts to make people smile or think or feel less alone. You never know

if you have posted something that turned someone's day around.

- Share your experiences with others - You can also remind people they are wonderful and valued by sharing your experiences and inviting them into these practices. No pressure, of course! Share what you're learned here and as long as you credit me, I think it's a wonderful way to be in service to community.

- Let others know you're there for them - Just letting people know you're available to help or to hear what they have to say is a beautiful way to serve others.

I want to also name that you should do these things for yourself first. You can't pour your service out well from an empty cup, after all. Make sure you are also caring for your brilliance before you start to give everyone else more than you might be able to sustain. Rainbows still need certain things to happen -- and you too need certain things to feel alive versus drained by service.

How to Work the Rainbow

While the practices above do move in an order where they build on each other, you can choose to skip around or to spend a lot of time in one place that calls to you. Though there are seven colors/ areas, I would not recommend doing all of them in one week. This is meant to be an extended exploration and one that can help you slowly emerge through places of stuckness or places of confusion. And to be clear, though there is a place to recognize your brilliance, you are already there. This is not a practice of goal setting. It's about emerging. As a rainbow drops from the sky when all conditions are right, you will too. From cloud to ground, from side to side, from ocean to vast blue sky.

Chapter 6

Rituals to Iris

I wish there were clear texts that might point to how Iris was worshipped in the past, but I have not been able to piece together much. What I can say is that from the practices I have seen for other Greek deities, these rituals are likely to be similar. To me this poses a question, however: do we strive to emulate the past or do we strive to find something new for the future? I personally believe the godds understand humans are continuously finding themselves in new times and in new contexts. As such, humans are going to interpret things via the lens they have in that moment.

Perhaps it's wise to begin with the types of rituals you might use with Iris. But this list might not include your idea, so remember this is just a starting point. In my experience, I call on Iris for:

- Writing
- Creative help
- Signs and messages to answer questions or guide my direction
- To remember beauty after storms
- Understanding service
- Communication

One of the things I like to keep in mind is that She is a go-between for the godds. So, when petitioning Her or calling out to Her, I might be calling on other godds for aid too. At the same time, I think Iris is capable of fulfilling desires too. While I can certainly appreciate detailed and complex rituals, my current method of magickal practice is focused more on intention versus frills. With that in mind, I offer you some direction and invite you to add your own creative energy.

Planning a Ritual to Iris

(Disclaimer: I think of absolute correspondences as being limiting. I also find spells with detailed lists of ingredients to be overwhelming and distracting. I will offer some ideas, but choose what works and is easily available to you.) Things you might use:

- Art supplies
- Candles of all colors
- Offerings
- A crystal that can refract and reflect light
- Rainbow colored yarn
- Anything you need to create magickal space
- Irises
- Rainbow colored items
- Paper
- Pens
- Water
- Pitcher
- Incense

My relationship with Iris has taught me that since She is a traveler, She can be anywhere at any time. If this is the case, I do not hold myself to any particular time of day or of the week. Unlike Aphrodite and other godds, She doesn't appear to have a day of celebration. The most common ritual to use for Iris is petitioning for help from the godds, and since this is likely something that is most useful to most people, I offer this to you.

Petitioning the Godds

For this ritual, I suggest finding a way to be in a space where you can be undisturbed. I also invite you to prepare ahead of time with what you are asking. I find it better to carefully consider what you are asking before entering the ritual space. And read this through a few times before you plan and complete the ritual. I also hold that Greek rituals often included a lot of preparation. As such, I encourage you to set up the sacred space with whatever you need to create a circle and call on the elements. You might set up an altar to Iris or you might choose to surround yourself with Iris flowers.

I encourage you to cleanse in some way that makes sense for you. This might be a bath right before the ritual or it might be washing of your face and hands. While you are cleansing, not only remove what you do not want to bring into the space, but also make room for the intention you are bringing to the ritual.

Think about what you are asking of the godds. What is the reason behind it? Is there any hesitation? Are there any adjustments you need to make? Are you asking the right question? Are you asking the truest question? Once you have that question in your mind and you are cleansed, come to the ritual space and prepare with a circle, calling in elements, and any other pieces you need to create a strong container for the working. And then call out to Iris. You might use the invocation in Chapter 3 or you might allow your intuition to guide you to what is right for this moment. Or you may have worked on an invocation for a while before the ritual -- it's completely up to you.

Once you feel Her presence in the space, I encourage you to sit and talk with Her. Call Her energy forward to you, as though She was sitting or standing across from you. You might take a crystal and hold it up to light to bring a rainbow down onto the floor as you do this. Sit with Her and let Her know what you are asking of Her and of the godds. Let Her know what it means to you and how it would impact your life. Allow Her to know your feelings and your motivations, as the more honest you are, the more accurately She can relay the message. When you are completely clear about what and why you are asking something of a godd, the more it shows your commitment.

This part of the ritual doesn't have to take long, but you might offer up the message and then wait to make sure there isn't anything more you need to say before you release Iris and open your circle. During this sort of ritual, I encourage you to say what you need to say, but then let go of what happens next. Let Iris travel and let the godds deliberate. Over the time after the ritual, I would encourage you to keep an eye out for messages and for the things that might tell you that you have sent a petition that will be answered.

Continue to make offerings to Iris as you can and as you will, because it's a relationship, after all. It's not just about asking for things and waiting for them. What might you offer in return?

Chapter 7

Cultivating a Relationship with Her

At this point of your journey, it is likely you have had some magical and mystical experiences. You have likely already had some places where you have heard messages and even begun to notice the presence of Iris in your life. As such, you may be interested in cultivating a relationship with Her. Before we begin this process, I want to offer some things to keep in mind. While not everyone feels the same way about building relationships with deities, I want to offer some that I have found helpful.

First things first, I had a teacher who once said that how you treat one relationship is how you treat all relationships. When I first heard this, it sounded a little too simple. After all, every relationship is different, so it's likely to not be true at all. It's more likely that how you treat one relationship is not how you treat all of them. But as a priestess of Iris, I stopped to hear what was being said.

Not all relationships are the same, true. But all relationships need attention. Even in this moment, I can think about my relationships with deities and the attention I offer to them. I feel closer to those who I devote more time to and I feel less close to those I only wave to from time to time. In the overall scheme of relationships, the more attention I devote, the more the relationship works for me. While this is what is said of humans, I believe this to be true of deities too. The more I spend time with Iris, the more messages I receive. The more I follow the messages I hear, the more I feel Her in my life.

So, why say all of this? Well, I say this because relationships take time. And it's easy to get frustrated when you're first working with a deity and it doesn't feel powerful all the time. I'm going to make sure you're building a strong foundation for your relationship so you know you are doing all you can. And, to be fair, just as with humans, some deity relationships don't work out the way we imagine them to work out.

Kinds of Deity Relationships

The best way I can describe relationships with the divine or mysterious ones is to remember there are different ways we are drawn to each other.

- The deity that jumps in your face
- The deity that you seem to be drawn to
- The deity you work with for a certain purpose
- The deity you 'have' to work with

(These are the most common scenarios I've experienced or heard of.)

You may have been thinking about Iris and then found this book and then realized you needed to be in a relationship. You may have been drawn to Iris so you started seeking information about Her. You may want to work with Iris because of a quality She offers. You may have to work with Iris for a project or a class.

All of these are valid and wonderful reasons. All of these are legitimate. But not all of these require the same sort of focus. For example, when you work with a deity for a certain purpose or project, it is wise to put enough attention for the relationship to be reciprocal, but you don't have to go on about your relationship forever.

When you're called to a deity or they call to you, I think it wise to give as much of your attention as you can. That seems kind, compassionate, and caring. It also recognizes that you are not the only part of the equation. I bring this to the forefront so you can be clear, again, about your expectations. What are you seeking from this relationship? What do you think a deity is supposed to do? What do you think you are supposed to do in return? The more you can figure this out, the more easily you can create a delightful and meaningful practice.

How to Give Attention

When I was first starting out in witchcraft, I read every book I could on how to do it right. Back then, I didn't have the access folks do now to all of the books, so it wasn't overly challenging. But now, with all of the books available, it can be overwhelming to know if you are doing something right. I'm going to let you in on a secret -- there is no right way to do things. There is your way.

Often, at this point of thinking about deity, someone will ask about working with deities that are not of your genetic or ancestral background. Here's my thought on that, knowing full well that conversations are nuanced and individual experiences and opinions vary.

If a godd calls to you, I think you should answer, no matter what pantheon they are from and whether they look like you. That said, I think this is a personal practice that you should explore on your own. Find out what the deity has to say to you. You may find it's just a message that you need to keep for yourself. Or you might find they want to have a deeper relationship with them. In that case, I would seek out someone who is from a tradition or group that honors that deity. Ask them what you might be able to do, who you might be able to study with, etc. And realize that even if you do everything 'right' in working with a deity, people can still have opinions and feel that you're out of integrity.

This is not to say you shouldn't listen to others. However, I think doing something out of truly wanting a relationship is fine, but becomes problematic when it turns into taking from a tradition or culture, or saying you're an expert without study or dedicated practice.

Also, while I know the idea of working with a deity from a

non-living tradition is something that seems to be okay in most pagan circles, I would also offer there are ways to give back to currently active groups or historical societies to ensure your deities or pantheon are well supported for the future.

As Starhawk once noted, *"I define cultural appropriation as 'Taking the gifts of the ancestors without a commitment to their descendants.'"* I agree. And I also think it's as simple as good manners to reciprocate blessings in some way.

With all of this in mind, giving attention to Iris can take a number of forms. I offer a few so that you have a starting point, versus a To Do list. I notice the way I interact with Iris follows sort of the same pattern as other relationships I've had in the past. Very close and caring at first, but then it got a little too relaxed and I had to get back on track to recommit.

When something is important, the coming back is vital. You are human and you will forget what you promised. But you can come back. You can always come back. You might begin and come back to:

Altars

One of the most common ways to bring attention to Iris is to create an altar. When I was first starting to build a relationship to Her, I found a card with Her image on it and used that as the focal point. It was a goddess with a long rainbow background and a pitcher. To me, this started to build in my mind what She continues to look like for me. On this altar I collected rainbow things and left offerings of pictures of rainbows and spells. Today, I have a statue of Her alongside a neon rainbow light to make it a bit more modern and fun.

And I'm sure the altar will continue to change in time. This altar is not as large or as filled as other altars I have and this seems to work for the moment. There are times and years when I have had larger altars to Her, and I imagine I will follow the cycles of my relationship with Her.

Devotional time

Just as with any relationship, it is wise to set aside devoted time to be with your special being. This might look like putting a 'date' time on your calendar or having a certain day of the week where they get special attention. During this time, you can choose to do other things, or you can simply sit with them in your mind or altar.

This allows you to bring yourself to the conversation as you are, even if you are upset. You can speak with Iris and you can listen to see what She has to say. You can wait to feel Her presence, go into a trance to meet with Her again, or simply do something that you think She might enjoy. As your relationship grows stronger, you will notice you can understand what She might like and you will move into a devotional space that is highly personal.

Nature walks

Since rainbows arrive from the sky (though crystals can bring them from outside sunlight), I focus on going out into nature to meet with Iris. Though it's not every day that I see rainbows, there is something about being in the wild that allows me to better connect with the wordless divine.

Just by being present in the outdoors, especially after rain, I feel this opens me up to the possibility of a gift from the clouds. I am inviting in a perfect moment when things are aligned and I can truly see what is around me. I can listen to messages, I can look for messages in the water and in the sky, as well as in other easy-to-miss places.

Other ideas for expanding awareness and traveling

That said, for those who are unable to access nature or might have troubles physically navigating it, looking at scenes online or going to these places in a meditation is just as effective. Looking out a window has been special for me when I've had to stay indoors. Listening to nature sounds can also bring me to the ocean, to the woods, or to a stormy night.

Art

I believe that Iris is a goddess of expression and communication. As such, it makes sense to me to use art as a way to communicate with Her. Bring messages of the human(s) to the godd(s). From collage with old magazine pictures to painting and drawing, you can bring all the colors of the rainbow into your life and heart.

You can create places of focus or new images of Iris that work for you. While She is often portrayed as a very white woman, I am certain the godds are not bound by human interpretation and limitation of imagination. You might create the vision of Iris you find in your trance or in your heart. You can bring that together as part of an altar, a spell working or some other focal point that allows you to feel connected.

Meditation and reflection

I've already mentioned the idea of meditations and I do feel these are important places to bring Iris into your consciousness a bit more. Plus, they're easy to do anywhere and require no special equipment beyond imagination.

If you're a person who feels trance or meditation don't work well for you, I would invite you to suspend disbelief for the moment. Pretend as though it is possible. Act as though anything were possible. When you can do this, you will open up to experiences that create more wonder and offer more grace.

The way you experience meditation is the way you experience it. There is no right or wrong way. You might see colors and shapes and people, or you might just feel something in your heart or gut. You can also simply bring yourself to a more grounded and open state and then wait to see what happens. It might begin by stating to yourself: I am meeting with Iris to hear what Her messages are. From there, you can do a progressive relaxation (as we did in the beginning of this book) or you might want to do something that's a little more Iris-themed.

One of the trance inductions I learned in Reclaiming Witchcraft is the rainbow induction. This is a method of progressive relaxation that enables your mind to let go of what came before and enter into a new space and state. All you need to do is to close your eyes (if that feels good to you) and allow your mind to settle. You might feel your body against the floor or chair or bed. You might slow your breathing or just notice how you are breathing.

Once you feel a little more settled, begin to imagine you are within a white cloud. This cloud is safe and warm and soft. It surrounds you and holds you.

The longer you are in this cloud, the more you begin to notice that it turns the color of red. The color of apples, strawberries, and cherries. The energy of beginnings and endings.

And slowly the cloud shifts and moves into the color orange. The color of persimmons and oranges and sunsets. The energy of heat and passion.

As this moves through your body, the cloud shifts into yellow. The colors of lemons and the middle of daisies and the freshest daffodils. The energy of newness and possibility.

And slowly the cloud shifts and moves into green. The new grass, the wide leaves, the ferns, and the evergreens. The energy of life bursting and blooming.

From there, the cloud turns to blue, surrounding you in the color of skies and birds and robin eggs. The energy of waters and the flow of life.

And the cloud moves into the color indigo, the deepest color of night and the background of stars. The energy of mystery and the movement of galaxies.

Finally, the cloud shifts into violet, the color of irises that grow upon burial mounds. The energy of returning.

Allow yourself to be in this space and this place of all the colors in one and resting on a cloud from which you can journey out to meet again with Iris....
(And you can leave time to be in this space.)
And then find a way to return the way you came, moving more quickly through each color of that cloud, from violet to indigo, from blue to green, from yellow to orange and back to red. Come back to this place, this time, this moment where you remember all that you need to remember.

You can also begin to make up different meditations that will bring you to the place where Iris is for you. This might be a temple or it might be Her place beside Hera, or some other secret place. Your relationship will emerge and you will know what's right for you.

Journaling

Since Iris is the messenger of the godds, it makes sense that you might connect with Her through writing. I find that writing after magickal experiences helps me remember them and eventually integrate the experience into my life. This can look like writing things down after trances or after you are in devotion with Iris. You can create a place where you also write things to Her, leave Her notes, and wait to see how She responds.

A practice could look like: Writing out a question in black and using other colors to answer as though Iris was holding the pen. I find this most effective when I am channeling or aspecting Iris.

Without getting into a long explanation of aspecting, this is a practice of taking the divine into your body as a devotional act. This is an opportunity for the divine to be embodied, while also being an opportunity to see the world through a deity's eyes.

A simple way to do this practice is to create a poem or some sort of invocation to Iris. You can do this and then say that out loud in order to call to Her and to invite Her into your body. As you repeat the invocation or poem over and over, you can begin to gather up the parts of your awareness that you are moving aside for the moment.

I usually collect them into an energetic ball and then push them down into the ground with a breath. The space that is left is where the divine enters and has a chance to move around. Once I feel Iris in my body, I can look at the paper with the question and She will consider how She might answer it. It doesn't always work to have Her with a task, but sometimes it will when I leave a clear question and my poem or invocation is not a rushed plea.

When the divine is done or when the human body is ready to let go, I start to breathe in the parts I dropped down into the earth, which pushes the divine out of the body. As that happens, I give thanks to Iris and I give thanks to Her wisdom.

I invite this to be a short session at first since aspecting is a deep working that requires repetition and practice. A way to make sure things aren't too long is to set a timer that will ring when you need to get out of the aspecting.

Chants and Prayers

I am a tremendous fan of making things up in the moment, but not everyone is that keen on doing so. After all, when you're first meeting someone, you likely want to make a good impression, so you may need to spend a little more time on preparing what you want to say.

When working with Iris, writing chants, songs, and prayers for Her is a great way to bring Her more fully into your life -- and to give a gift to Her. It will also begin to create a working only the two of you share, which will strengthen your connection.

You can choose to create something that rhymes -- or not. You can also choose to use tunes you already know, while writing new lyrics. Or you can go back to old texts to see what is already there and read those aloud.

I personally find that invocations are a great place to create connection and authentic relating. I suggest getting into a calm and grounded state, perhaps even setting magickal space in the way that works for you. You might sit in the space and decide what qualities of Iris are important or most present to you in the moment. You might think of stories or you might think of visuals and build from there.

For me, since it's a personal relationship and not a public working, I would relate to Her as I would a friend. For example, I might create an invocation that speaks of Her strength, noting that I wish I had Her strength or the ease She has in traveling between worlds.

I would point out things I love and then reflect on my own growth and commitment. In doing so, I am reflecting and from there I might ask for guidance or support, if needed. Or I might just write an invocation as a love letter to Iris. I might tell Her all the things I think She's wonderful at and all the things I admire. From here, I can bask in that glow and enjoy healing that comes from offering gratitude.

Research

While I'm sure you will find more ways to give attention to Iris as you get to know Her in your own way, doing research on Her is a great way to get to know Her. Even if you simply read other practitioner accounts, you can find new facets to explore. You can see what others are saying. And if you're anything like me, you will notice your relationship is different from others. And that's okay. Or you might find a similar experience that you thought was weird, but apparently is shared by others.

My hope is that Iris is studied more and that Her service becomes an inspiration in more circles. She is not just a lady-in-waiting; She is a messenger who was trusted with the most important messages.

When Relationships Don't Work

Because this will likely come up, I wanted to bring in a short section about what to do when relationships don't go the way you think they should. Perhaps you have done the things you said you would do. You have been clear about what you expect. And still, you just don't feel the presence of the divine.

Because the patriarchal society is so ingrained in human psyches, it is common to immediately wonder what you've done wrong. This happens not only in relationships with deities, but also in relationships with other humans. I want to remind you: you might not be doing anything wrong. You might be showing up, doing personal work, paying attention, journaling, meditating at an altar, and calling out to Iris. But if She is not showing up, it might be that the relationship is not meant to be at that moment. And that's okay. You can still decide to show up and be there. You can still have a cordial relationship with Her and what She means to you.

However, if you begin to feel resentful or upset, then perhaps you need to step away from that relationship for a while. Again, it might not be the right time. But I truly believe that if you're called to Her, you will come back. She will come back to you too.

Practice: Dedication Ritual

For those who are ready to commit themselves to Iris or who are willing to dedicate themselves for a certain time period of study, this dedication ritual can help.

What you need:

7-day white candle
Permanent markers of many colors or paints
White cloth or scarf
Picture of a rainbow

Since this is a ritual, I would encourage you to begin with setting sacred space in the way that you do. For some, this looks like cleansing, grounding, and casting a circle and calling in the elements. Since this is your dedication ritual, decide what works best for you.

At that point, I would invite in Iris, placing the rainbow picture in the middle of the circle. I would write an invocation about what I see in Her and what I want to see in myself. I might talk about my intention for the ritual and the work together, while putting the white scarf around my shoulders or neck.

From there, I would trance into a space where you get to meet with Iris to get information about what the work together will include or what I would need to know about a formal commitment. I would also have a conversation with Her about the length of time if I haven't already decided on a timeline.

Once out of that trance or mediation, I would decorate the candle with the markers or paints, showcasing what I am dedicating to or promising. I might use symbols or words, depending on what makes the most sense to me (and what allows me to remember these vows). I would hold the candle to bring the energy of Iris into the candle. Once I felt Her in the candle, I would light it and make a statement of my dedication for the timeline I agreed to. I would leave the candle lit for a while and relight it for as many days as seemed appropriate. I could also replace the candle with a small tea light or LED candle to keep it shining through the dedication period. The scarf could then be used as an altarpiece or as something that is worn in rituals to Iris.

The time is right for this ritual when you are clear about why you are dedicating yourself. You could choose to do it immediately or you could choose to wait until you were sure.

For myself, I re-dedicate each year, for a year and a day. But the ritual is much simpler since we've done it many times before.

Conclusion

This might be the first time you've met Iris. Or perhaps you've heard of Her and wondered what She might have to offer your life and your heart. Maybe you got a strong message, emblazoned with meaning. Or perhaps the rainbow disappeared too quickly for interpretation.

No matter what you have experienced here, no matter what path calls you forward now, I want you to remember Iris often comes in forms you may not recognize. Or, better said, She comes in forms you do recognize, but you may not recognize it as Her. She is often there. She is there in the questions. She is there in the asking. She is there in the moments where all you can think is to scream at the godds.

I have screamed at the godds too. She is there in the laughter. She is there in the longing. She is there in the wide-open song that travels and arrives in a moment.

I invite you to listen.
I invite you to open.
I invite you to serve others and yourself.
I invite you to touch the clouds and feel the waters.
I invite you to pour water in her name.
I invite you to celebrate the way you radiate light, even from the most broken places.
I invite you to know you can travel to heavens and to underworlds and back again.

May this journey bless you and hold you.
May you look up and know home.
May the rainbows follow you and guide you in all of your days.

Hail Daughter of Sea and Cloud!
Hail Rainbow!
Hail Traveler!
Hail Messenger!
Hail Golden-Winged One!
Hail Iris!

Bibliography

Aeneid, Virgil
Catalogues of Women Fragments, Hesiod
The Iliad, Homer
Mythology, Edith Hamilton
Theogony, Hesiod (translated by Hugh Evelyn-White)

[Offerings to Iris information], Athen. xiv. p. 645; comp. Müller, Aegin. p. 170

https://elysiumgates.com/mt_olympus/histiris.html
https://goddessofpurple.neocities.org/deities/cheatsheet1.html
http://www.rwaag.org/iris
http://www.theoi.com/Pontios/Iris.html

MOON
BOOKS

PAGANISM & SHAMANISM

What is Paganism? A religion, a spirituality, an alternative
belief system, nature worship? You can find support for all these
definitions (and many more) in dictionaries, encyclopaedias, and
text books of religion, but subscribe to any one and the truth will
evade you. Above all Paganism is a creative pursuit, an encounter
with reality, an exploration of meaning and an expression of the
soul. Druids, Heathens, Wiccans and others, all contribute their
insights and literary riches to the Pagan tradition. Moon Books
invites you to begin or to deepen your own encounter, right here,
right now.
If you have enjoyed this book, why not tell other readers by
posting a review on your preferred book site.

Recent bestsellers from Moon Books are:

Journey to the Dark Goddess
How to Return to Your Soul
Jane Meredith
Discover the powerful secrets of the Dark Goddess and
transform your depression, grief and pain into healing
and integration.
Paperback: 978-1-84694-677-6 ebook: 978-1-78099-223-5

Shamanic Reiki
Expanded Ways of Working with Universal Life Force Energy
Llyn Roberts, Robert Levy
Shamanism and Reiki are each powerful ways of healing; together,
their power multiplies. *Shamanic Reiki* introduces techniques to
help healers and Reiki practitioners tap ancient healing wisdom.
Paperback: 978-1-84694-037-8 ebook: 978-1-84694-650-9

Pagan Portals – The Awen Alone
Walking the Path of the Solitary Druid
Joanna van der Hoeven
An introductory guide for the solitary Druid, *The Awen Alone* will
accompany you as you explore, and seek out your own place
within the natural world.
Paperback: 978-1-78279-547-6 ebook: 978-1-78279-546-9

A Kitchen Witch's World of Magical Herbs & Plants
Rachel Patterson
A journey into the magical world of herbs and plants, filled with
magical uses, folklore, history and practical magic. By popular
writer, blogger and kitchen witch, Tansy Firedragon.
Paperback: 978-1-78279-621-3 ebook: 978-1-78279-620-6

Medicine for the Soul
The Complete Book of Shamanic Healing
Ross Heaven
All you will ever need to know about shamanic healing and how to become your own shaman...
Paperback: 978-1-78099-419-2 ebook: 978-1-78099-420-8

Shaman Pathways – The Druid Shaman
Exploring the Celtic Otherworld
Danu Forest
A practical guide to Celtic shamanism with exercises and techniques as well as traditional lore for exploring the Celtic Otherworld.
Paperback: 978-1-78099-615-8 ebook: 978-1-78099-616-5

Traditional Witchcraft for the Woods and Forests
A Witch's Guide to the Woodland with Guided Meditations and Pathworking
Mélusine Draco
A Witch's guide to walking alone in the woods, with guided meditations and pathworking.
Paperback: 978-1-84694-803-9 ebook: 978-1-84694-804-6

Wild Earth, Wild Soul
A Manual for an Ecstatic Culture
Bill Pfeiffer
Imagine a nature-based culture so alive and so connected, spreading like wildfire. This book is the first flame...
Paperback: 978-1-78099-187-0 ebook: 978-1-78099-188-7

Naming the Goddess
Trevor Greenfield
Naming the Goddess is written by over eighty adherents and
scholars of Goddess and Goddess Spirituality.
Paperback: 978-1-78279-476-9 ebook: 978-1-78279-475-2

Shapeshifting into Higher Consciousness
Heal and Transform Yourself and Our World with Ancient
Shamanic and Modern Methods
Llyn Roberts
Ancient and modern methods that you can use every day to
transform yourself and make a positive difference in the world.
Paperback: 978-1-84694-843-5 ebook: 978-1-84694-844-2

Readers of ebooks can buy or view any of these bestsellers by
clicking on the live link in the title. Most titles are published in
paperback and as an ebook. Paperbacks are available in traditional
bookshops. Both print and ebook formats are available online.

Find more titles and sign up to our readers' newsletter at
http://www.johnhuntpublishing.com/paganism
Follow us on Facebook at https://www.facebook.com/MoonBooks
and Twitter at https://twitter.com/MoonBooksJHP